Seeing Jesus

EYEWITNESS ASSEMBLIES

Contents

About the author

After a decade in publishing, Gill Thorniley is now a full-time freelance writer. Previously she has been a nurse, civil servant, administrator, cleaner and gardener. She has spent twenty years being involved, in a voluntary capacity, with children in schools, playgroups and Sunday groups and has been a childminder. Gill also remembers the questions she asked as a child, and hopes, through her writing, to provide a context for the current generation to explore these issues. Gill is married with two teenage children and lives in the Midlands.

Introduction

This book is a complete resource for those involved in planning primary school assemblies. Each story contains a way in, ideas for performing the story, a prayer and extension ideas for the classroom. For each story there is both a general theme and one with a Christian perspective on the story, so that the assembly leaders can choose the one most appropriate for their setting.

These stories give eyewitness accounts of Jesus' life from his birth to his post-resurrection appearances. They are drawn from the biblical accounts, and references are given, but political and cultural information is included to make them more accessible to today's children.

The witnesses whose stories are told do not all find Jesus acceptable, and the conflicts and struggles brought about by his ministry are explored. The book will help children understand why Jesus and his teachings had such a dramatic effect, causing some people to leave everything to follow him, and some to seek his death. The stories give an account of what Christians believe Jesus did while on earth, and as such would augment the teaching of Christianity in Religious Education lessons.

Mary's story:

Jesus is born

References: Matthew 1:18-24; Luke 1–2

General theme: Coping with things we don't understand.
Christian theme: God has a plan for Jesus.
Way in: Has anyone seen a baby? What are babies like, what can they do?
Introduction: This is a story about a young girl called Mary. She has just had a baby and is learning to cope with things that she doesn't understand.

Story

My little baby's sleeping now. Be careful or you'll wake him. He's tiny and so helpless. It's hard to believe that he's different from any other baby. He's perfect, smelling like all new babies smell, and his little hands and feet are all wrinkled. He's making little baby noises in his sleep. Just like any baby. But I know he's not just any baby.

I know what you're thinking: every mother thinks that her baby is special. But not every mother sees an angel. There I was, sitting at home, preparing food for our evening meal, when suddenly there was this shiny being in the room with me. I just knew that this being was an angel; well it definitely wasn't human! And I was scared.

I was trying to decide whether to run away or hide, or maybe both, when the angel spoke to me. He said, 'Don't be afraid, Mary!' He knew my name. He knew a lot more than that. He told me that I was going to have a baby boy, who was going to be very special. He told me that my boy would be a king.

Well, we're not royal; I don't belong to the royal family and neither does Joseph, my fiancé. I said, 'I can't be expecting a baby, Joseph and I aren't married yet.' But the angel said that that was what was going to make this baby special. It would be God's own son. So I said to the angel that if God wanted this baby, then I would have it.

Joseph was angry when I told him about the baby, because he knew he wasn't the father. I thought that he would leave me and take a new wife. But God told Joseph in a dream that he should still marry me, because it was all part of God's plan. So then Joseph got excited too, and he's looked after me so well over the last nine months.

And then at the last minute, the governor decides we must all go back to the towns our families came from and register there. So at nine months pregnant, I've had to travel all the way to Bethlehem, with Joseph. For two days I've been sitting on a donkey, who only walked when he felt like it. It's not much fun sitting on a wobbly donkey for hours, especially not when your tummy is as big as mine. At night we joined with other travellers and slept as well as we could, usually in the courtyard of an inn.

When we arrived last night I was so tired. I could feel that the baby would be born soon. Joseph was worried because everywhere was busy and full, and we needed somewhere to stay. We kept being turned away from the inns. Joseph joked and said it was probably because I'm so big with the baby that they didn't think I'd fit through the doors! I could see that he was worried though, because he frowned and bit his lip as we went through the busy streets.

Eventually one innkeeper said that although his inn was full, we could sleep in the stable block, where we could be warm and a bit more private than in the courtyard. It was so good to get off that donkey and stop moving. I hardly even noticed how dark and smelly it is here in the stable. The animals were noisy and excited, but I didn't mind. At last I could lay down and rest. Joseph unpacked the few things we'd brought with us, while I lay down.

It was hard work when my baby was born, and I wanted my mum. I expect I made a lot of noise. I don't really remember much, until Joseph handed me the baby and said, 'Look, at our son, Jesus. He's perfect.' And I looked down at his wrinkled little face and wondered. He looked so ordinary. A little baby, born in a smelly stable. Had I imagined the angel? Could Jesus really be that special?

I fell asleep wondering. And then later that night, the shepherds came. The first ones came bursting in, breathless from running in from the fields. Then more came, with the last ones creeping in, quiet and shy. They didn't know why they had come. They didn't know what to expect. They said, 'We've come to see the baby.'

They'd been looking after their sheep out in the dark fields, when suddenly a shining angel was there with them. They were frightened, just like I'd been when I'd seen an angel, but the angel had told them not to be afraid. He said that he had good news for them, because a special boy, who would save people, had been born in Bethlehem.

The angel had told them where they could find us, and now here they were, all excited and out of breath, all talking at once and gazing down at Jesus. They were excited because they had found us, and everything was as the angel had said.

Finally, they left, making a great noise, singing praises to God. Joseph and I just looked at one another in amazement. We were right: Jesus *is* special and God *does* have a plan for him.

Performance

A baby doll and carry cot can be used as props. There could be a display of things needed for a baby – nappies, bath, bottles, bedding, toys, etc.

Prayer

Dear God,
We pray for all those who look after babies. Help them to care for the babies and to love them. Please bless all babies, because every baby is special to you.
Amen.

The children could pray for babies using an action prayer; for example, please help all babies when they cry (mime crying), when they are feeding (mime feeding), etc.

General theme

Mary had a new baby to look after; what do babies need? What do they do most?
Mary didn't understand why God wanted her to have Jesus, or what Jesus would do. Are there things that we don't understand? How do we cope when things happen that we don't understand? The Bible says that Mary remembered everything and waited until things were revealed to her.

Christian theme

Mary trusted God and believed that he had a plan for her and Jesus. Why do you think Mary trusted God? (She knew him through prayer and scriptures.)
Do you think we can trust God?
Mary saw an angel. What other ways are there of finding out God's plan for us? (These might include praying, reading the Bible, discovering what talents God has given us.)

Extension ideas

1. Look at the things that babies need – food, water, sleep, warmth, love. Using baby catalogues, cut out equipment, clothes and toys and make a collage.
2. Practise looking after a baby doll.
3. Have a mother bring in a baby, show it and ask the mother to talk about her experiences with her baby.
4. God had a plan. Get the children to make a plan for an activity, and then do it; for example, make a plan for cooking biscuits and then cook them.

David's story:

Jesus is baptised

References: Matthew 3:1-17; Luke 3:1-22

General theme: Saying sorry; being forgiven.
Christian theme: John recognises that Jesus is sent from God.
Way in: Today is all about saying sorry. Have you ever had to say sorry?
Today is about a baptism. Have you ever been to a baptism or christening? What happens?
Introduction: This is a story about a man we'll call David, who went to hear John the Baptist speak, and who wanted to say sorry to God.

Story   I've done some bad things in my time. It doesn't matter what, it's all behind me now. But I know what it's like to feel all wrong inside, knowing that you've hurt people, let them down, told lies. I still get things wrong now. I talk before I think, and sometimes I get very angry. But I know what to do now. Thanks to John and Jesus.

Mind you, when I first saw John I laughed at him. It makes me go red now when I think about it. He did look silly though. He was very skinny with long hair and you could hardly see his face because of his bushy beard. His clothes were made from camel's hair, tied round with a leather belt. He spent most of his time wandering in the desert round here and, to be honest, he looked half mad.

I went up with some of my mates to hear him shouting at people – we'd heard he ranted and raved. We thought we'd go and make fun of him, it'd be a good laugh. He was standing by the edge of the River Jordan, at the ford, where it's not too deep. There were about 20 people round him: some were listening to him, some were laughing at him.

The first thing I noticed was that he didn't seem to care that some folk were laughing at him. I was still going to call him some rude names and then run away. But just then, he called out, 'Turn away from all the bad things you've done, because God's kingdom is very near.'

Funnily enough, before we'd come I'd been thinking about some of the bad things I'd done, wondering why I got things so wrong sometimes and what I could do about it. So I stood and listened, standing in the hot sun, by the muddy river. John seemed to know how I felt. He said we should say sorry; that we could start again; and that God would forgive us.

Some of the crowd called out, 'What should we do now?'

John said, 'Share your clothes and food with those who don't have enough. If you're big and strong, like soldiers, don't knock people about and take money from them. Don't lie.'

I got interested in what John was saying. He seemed to know what it felt like to do things wrong, but to want to do things right. Although he looked so strange, what he said made sense, and it excited me. He said that God's kingdom was very near and that things were going to change. Someone important was coming, someone much better and closer to God than John.

That got me thinking, all right. Maybe this someone would chase the Romans out of our land, stop the rich stealing money from the poor and put things right again. This was something I could understand. I realised that I trusted John.

He said that if we wanted a fresh start in our lives that we should come into the river with him, and that he would pray for us and baptise us. The water wouldn't make our insides clean, but it would show people that we were serious and wanted to say sorry to God. I wanted to go forward, but I thought my mates would laugh, until I saw that they'd gone up ahead of me.

I followed on. I waded waist-high into the water. When I got to John, he lowered me into the water so that it completely covered me, and he prayed to God. He asked God to forgive me, and to help me to lead a good life. I coughed and spluttered as the water splashed over me, but I felt like singing. It was like a new beginning. Even though the water was dirty and muddy, I felt cleaner than I had in years.

I got to the side of the river, climbed out and rejoined my friends. I thought I was last, but as I was trying to wring the water out of my clothes, everyone suddenly became quiet. I looked up. John was at the water's edge now, because everyone had been baptised. Everyone except one man, who was pointing out to the river and asking John to baptise him. John shook his head and said, 'No. I can't baptise you.'

I was shocked, what had this man done that was so bad that he couldn't be forgiven? But then John said, 'It's the wrong way round. You should be baptising me. You've done nothing wrong.' The man insisted, saying that God wanted it, and therefore John should baptise him. John finally agreed. They walked into the water together and John poured water over him, exactly as he had done to me. Someone said his name was Jesus.

As John prayed to God, something special happened. I can only say that it felt like heaven opened up. Something like a dove came down onto Jesus, but it wasn't a dove, it was God's spirit. And I heard a voice say, 'You are my son, and I am pleased with you.' It was very quiet apart from that voice. We all knew something different and wonderful had happened. Was Jesus the important person John had told us about?

It's been some months now since John baptised me. I often listen to him, and try to do what he tells me. Jesus is preaching now, and some say that he can do miracles. Maybe one day I'll follow him.

Performance

During the story bleach can be used on stained clothes or on water containing food dye to show things becoming clean again and to explain how forgiveness works: our dirty deeds are cleaned away.

Prayer

Dear God,
Sometimes we do and say wrong things. We hurt you and we hurt those around us. We are sorry for all the times we have got things wrong. Please forgive us and help us to get things right. Amen.

As a group the children could make a list of all the wrong things they do and say sorry to God for those, and then make a second list of all the right things they can do and ask God's help to do these more often.

General theme

Is it all right to do something wrong if we think we can get away with it?
What things do you think are wrong?
How do you feel when you do something wrong and don't say sorry?
If someone says sorry to you for something, how should you respond?

Christian theme

Why did David trust John? How did he know that John was speaking the truth?

Had Jesus done anything wrong? Why do you think he was baptised? (To identify with us.)

Are there some things that people do that we find hard to forgive? Does God forgive them?

Extension ideas

1. John gave his listeners some ideas on how to behave – don't steal, don't lie, etc. The children could draw up their own lists of do's and don'ts. They could then compare their lists to the Ten Commandments (see Exodus 20:1-17).

2. The children could make a picture or model of John using wool for hair and fake fur for his clothes.

3. We have been looking at how *people* can change, try some experiments to help them grasp the concept: water can be water, ice or vapour; cake ingredients change when mixed together and cooked.

4. The children could look at the different ways things can be made clean; for example, mistakes on paper can be rubbed out; clothes, cars and humans can be washed; germs can be killed with antiseptics or heat.

Simon Peter's story (1):

Jesus calls Simon Peter

References: Luke 5:1-11; Matthew 4:18-22; Mark 1:16-20

General theme: Making decisions.
Christian theme: Peter responds to Jesus' call on his life.
Way in: People do all kinds of jobs. What jobs can you think of?
Introduction: This story is about a man called Simon Peter. He was a fisherman until he met Jesus, who gave him a new job.

Story Sometimes you just have to admit you don't know everything. I've been a fisherman all my life, and I thought I knew everything there was to know about fishing but one day Jesus showed me something and changed my life.

Most of the time I enjoyed fishing: it can be a good life when the sun's shining and you're joking with your friends after a good catch, but it can get scary too out on the water when a storm gets up.

I was fed up that morning. We'd been working hard all night and hadn't caught a single fish. We'd come back to the shore and we were cleaning our nets. Just along the shore a new teacher called Jesus was speaking, surrounded by a crowd. The crowd got bigger and bigger. There must have been a couple of hundred people there at least. As the crowd got bigger, Jesus found it hard to stand where everyone could see him. Eventually there were so many people that he climbed into my boat. He asked me to take the boat out a little way, so that he could speak to the crowd from the lake.

Although I'd been listening to him, I was about to tell him where to get off. But, as I looked up at his face, there was something about him that stopped the rude words in my mouth. Somehow I found that I couldn't say no to Jesus. So although I was tired and hungry, I got back into the boat and pulled it out into the lake. My brother Andrew came too.

Jesus carried on talking to the crowd. He stood up in my boat, while I pulled it out. He was bobbing up and down with the movement of the waves, but it didn't seem to bother him.

The gaggle of people at the water's edge carried on listening to him. I listened too, as the waves splashed against the side of the boat and the sun got hotter and hotter. I found that even when he talked about difficult things, I could understand him.

When he finished he turned to me and said, 'Go further out into the lake, and let down your nets to catch fish.'

I said to him, 'Teacher, we've been out all night fishing. We know what we're doing and we've not caught a thing.' I was about to say to him that he may be a good teacher but he's no fisherman. But looking at him, I found myself saying, 'But because you've asked me, I'll let them down again.'

I didn't expect anything. I don't know why I did it really. There was just something about him that was different. So my brother, Andrew, and I went even further out into the lake and threw the nets overboard again. When we pulled the nets back up, they were full of fish! We had so many fish that the nets began to break!

We called to our friends, James and John, to come over with their boat and help us. Even with two boats and all of us heaving on the nets, we had problems getting all the fish on board. And when we did, the boats were so full that they began to sink.

James, John and Andrew began to row like mad to the shore. This was a catch like no other, and we didn't want to have to throw all those fish back in. Neither did we want to sink. I looked at Jesus sitting there calmly surrounded by all those wriggling, smelly fish, and realised he knew so much. I mean he's a carpenter, and yet he helps us land one of our biggest catches ever. There was something different about him, something special. I knelt down in front of him and said, 'I'm not good enough for you, Lord, you'd better leave me.'

But instead of agreeing, he said, 'Don't be scared. Follow me! From now on you'll be fishing for men.' He asked all of us that day to follow him: Andrew, James, John and me.

We pulled the boats up on to the shore, and then we left everything we had ever known and followed him. We didn't know what we were going to do. We just knew it was important to be with Jesus, and to do what he wanted us to do. We didn't know everything, but we had a feeling that maybe Jesus did. In one morning our lives had changed forever.

Performance The narrator could dress up as a fisherman and the space used could be dressed to look like the shore of a lake, with pictures and models of boats, real nets, fishing rods, fabric chairs, etc.

Prayer

Dear God,
We pray for all those at work. We pray especially for all those who help to provide our food: for farmers, fishers, cooks, factory workers and lorry drivers. We ask your blessing on them and on all those who work to provide for us.
Amen.

The children could write their own prayers on paper fish, which could then be caught up in a net to remind them that God knows our needs and cares about us.

General theme

What job would you like to do when you leave school?
Simon Peter had a choice to make in today's story. How do you decide when you have choices to make? (Is it right or wrong; will anyone get hurt; will I like it; etc.?)
How do you think Simon Peter felt when Jesus asked him to give up fishing and follow him?

Christian theme

Why do you think Simon Peter decided to leave everything and follow Jesus?
Can you think of people today who give up things to follow Jesus? (For example, monks and nuns, people whose family don't approve of them being Christians, etc.)
What does this tell us about following Jesus? (It's not always easy!)

Looking at choices we have to make. This could be a game with choices to which several answers are given, for the children to think through and decide.

Extension ideas

1. The children could take a closer look at choices through playing a game; for example, by using cards with questions on them which they have to answer, such as, 'If you found money on the street would you hand it in or take it?'
2. The children could make a fish mobile.
3. The children could make and play a fishing game, with paper fish with paperclips on them, and fishing rods with magnets.
4. The children could do a project on either fish (types of fish and their habitats, freshwater and sea water, and their life cycle) or on water (streams, rivers, lakes and seas). They could research and then write or paint a picture.

Anna's story:

Jesus goes to a wedding at Cana

Reference: John 2:1-11

General theme: Other people can help us sort out our problems.
Christian theme: Jesus surprises his friends by doing a miracle and showing that he is more than a teacher.
Way in: Have you ever been to a wedding? What was it like?
Introduction: Today's story is about Anna, who was a servant to a family in a town called Cana. Anna had a problem: something went very wrong at a wedding party.

Story

What a wedding that was! It could have been a real disaster. You haven't heard about it? Well let me tell you what happened.

I work for a family in a town called Cana. I cook and clean and help to keep the house running smoothly. I pride myself on getting everything just right. Well the son of the household was getting married. Everyone comes to the party of course, and we'd been busy for weeks, ordering food, dusting cobwebs, making new clothes. We thought we had everything ready . . .

On the day of the wedding, the son went to collect his bride from her parents' house. He brought her back to his house. It was a proper procession, with all their friends singing and dancing. Then both sets of parents gave them their blessing, and the party began.

We began to serve the food, and everyone was enjoying themselves. It was going really well. Then, when the party was in full swing, we discovered that we'd run out of wine! Not a drop left. The party was still going on, and no one was planning to go home yet. We'd got it wrong; we hadn't got enough wine! We began to panic because we didn't know what to do. When everyone found out, our master's family would be disgraced, and we'd be in trouble.

One of the guests, a woman called Mary, was standing nearby, and she noticed that we had a problem. She called her son over to tell him. At first, it didn't seem as though he was going to be much help. He said, 'Why are you telling me now?'

She must have believed he could do something though, because she said to us, 'Do whatever he tells you to.'

So we waited to see what would happen. This man, Jesus his name was, pointed to six stone jars that we usually use for washing water. He said, 'Fill the jars with water.'

It didn't seem very helpful, but no one had a better idea. Besides there was something about him that made us believe he could do something. So we did as he said. We filled the water jars to the top.

Then he said, 'Now take some out and take it to the chief steward.' The chief steward was the man that the bridegroom's family had put in charge of the party. It seemed like asking for trouble to take him water when he was expecting wine. But someone did as Jesus said, and we discovered as we poured it out that it wasn't water any more, but wine. None of us could understand this. We'd put in water, but we were now pouring out wine.

We took it to the chief steward. He tasted it and called to the bridegroom, 'Everyone else serves the best wine first, and then they bring out the stuff that's not so good. But you've saved the best to the end. Well done, my friend.' We couldn't believe what we had seen. The chief steward didn't know where the good wine had come from – but we did.

How did he do it? I mean, water went in, so water should have come out, shouldn't it?

Something very odd happened at that party. It seems that that man Jesus is someone special. We looked for him afterwards, but he was with his friends. They'd seen what had happened and it had changed how they acted around him. I mean, they'd been his friends before and they'd looked up to him. He was a teacher after all. But now things were different – even teachers can't turn water into wine. I don't think it was just the wine that was changed at that wedding.

Performance

The narrator and children could dress in party clothes. During the story water could be put into a container, which already had food colouring in it, and then poured out again, so that the audience could see the change of colour. The narrator would need to say that this is a trick, and that Jesus did not use a trick.

Prayer

Dear God,
Thank you for parties and celebrations. Thank you for party food and drink. Please help all those who don't have enough to eat to get all that they need.
Amen.

The children could draw a picture or write a poem about fun times, and then thank God for what is on their paper.

General theme

What parties or celebrations have you been to? What made them fun?

Anna had a problem. What do you do when you have problems? Anna was helped by Jesus. Who helps you when things go wrong? Do you help your friends when they have a problem? How do you help your friends?

Christian theme

This story was about a wedding. Why do you think people get married?

This story was about a miracle that Jesus performed. What is a miracle?

In this story water was changed into wine. Anna told us the disciples also changed. How do you think the disciples might have changed and why? (The disciples came to believe in Jesus as someone sent by God.)

Extension ideas

1. Have a party. The children could make invitations and food. Party games could be played.
2. The children could bring in pictures of weddings and other parties. They could make a collage or painting of a celebration or party food.
3. Have a procession with singing and dancing and lights. If appropriate a blessing could be said over the children, just as the bride and groom were blessed.
4. Lights were an important feature of the wedding procession. Look at the different types of light – sun, moon, stars, candles, torches, firelight, etc. Let the children look at how we use light. They could write a story where light plays an important role.

Michael's story:

Jesus tells a story (the Good Samaritan)

Reference: Luke 10:25-37

General theme: Helping others.

Christian theme: Jesus challenges the way people think.

Way in: Who likes stories? What's your favourite story?

Introduction: Jesus liked to tell people stories. Sometimes stories can help us to understand difficult things. Our story is about a man called Michael who heard Jesus tell a story. Michael is a scribe, a teacher who is used to answering questions.

Story

It's not often someone gets the better of me. I've spent years studying the Law, and people come to me to sort out arguments. I tell them what they should do. I have an answer for every question. At least I thought I did. I'm a bit confused since my conversation with Jesus.

Our religious Law is important to me. I try to keep all of the rules, and I know all of them, even the small ones that most people forget. That's why people come to me to sort out their problems. To find out what they should do, so that they don't upset God by breaking his rules.

I'd heard a lot about Jesus, and what I heard confused me. He did good things, healing people, talking about God and taking God seriously. But people were saying that he was breaking some of God's rules, working on our holy day, talking and eating with criminals and other bad people and forgiving people their sins, which is something only God can do. So what kind of man was he: good or bad? There was only one way to find out. I had to go and listen to him myself.

So one cloudy day, I set off to find Jesus and listen to him talk. I sat on the edge of the group around him. I didn't want to get too close in case people thought that I was with him. We sat down on the dusty ground while Jesus talked and told stories. As I listened, I played with the stones beneath my hands. All that

Jesus said made sense, and I agreed with it. But I was still confused. What about all those tales about him breaking God's laws? What kind of man was he really – good or bad?

I decided that I needed to test him to find out what sort of person he really was. When he stopped talking for a while, while he was eating some figs, I stood up and said, 'Teacher, what do I need to do to get to heaven?'

He looked over at me, and said, between mouthfuls, 'What does the Bible say?'

I already knew the answer to this. I said, 'The Bible says love God with all your heart, all your soul, all your strength and all your mind. And love your neighbour like you love yourself.'

Jesus wiped his hands of fig juice and said, 'You are right, do this and you will go to heaven.'

This was no good to me. Jesus had just got me to answer my own question, and then he agreed with me. I still didn't know whether he was good or bad.

So before he could talk to someone else, I asked him another question, 'And who is my neighbour?' Ha, I thought, you've got to answer this one, and then I'll know whether I can trust you or not.

To my surprise Jesus began to tell me a story. The crowd settled back happily; they liked Jesus' stories.

'Once upon a time, a man was going down the rocky road between Jerusalem and Jericho. On the way robbers came and attacked him. They took everything he had, even his clothes. They beat him up and then they ran away and left him, not caring whether he lived or died.

'Some time later a priest came down the road. He saw the man, bleeding by the roadside.'

Jesus paused and we waited to hear what the priest would do. If the man was dead and the priest touched him, he wasn't allowed to work in the Temple for a week. But surely the priest would help him.

Jesus continued, 'But he walked across to the other side of the road, and didn't stop. Later on still, a Levite came by. He went over and looked at the man.'

Jesus stopped again. We waited to hear what the Levite would do. He was a man who looked after all the religious buildings. Here was someone who would know the right thing to do.

Again Jesus continued, 'And then he went on his way without stopping. Even later a Samaritan came by—'

At this we all gasped. If the priest and the Levite hadn't helped, then the Samaritan would probably kick him some more. It's a long story, but we hate Samaritans and they hate us.

Jesus repeated, 'A Samaritan came by. He saw the man, and he felt sorry for him. He went over to him. He cleaned his wounds and bandaged them. He put the man onto his own donkey and took him to the nearest inn. All night he took care of the man. Morning came and he had to leave and go on his way. He gave the innkeeper enough money to look after the man for about eight weeks. He said to the innkeeper, "Take care of him. If it costs any more I will pay you on my way back."'

Jesus looked at me, 'This poor man who was attacked by robbers. Who do you think treated him like a neighbour?'

I knew the answer that he wanted, but I couldn't say it. I couldn't say that a Samaritan had done the right thing, when holy men hadn't. He was still looking at me, wanting an answer. Eventually I said, 'The man who looked after him.'

Jesus said to me, 'You go and do the same.'

And that was the end of it. Jesus started talking to someone else. I still don't know what to think. Was Jesus saying that the others were wrong, because they wanted to keep the rules and keep themselves clean, by not touching the man who was injured. They were doing the right thing. But I know if I was beaten up, I'd want someone like the Samaritan to come along and help me. Jesus is changing the way we look at things, and I still don't know if he's right or wrong. What do you think?

Performance

This could be performed as a mime, with the children taking specific parts, or with every child pretending to be the robbers, victim, priests and Samaritan as the story is told.

Prayer

Dear God,
Thank you for all those who help others. We thank you for those who look after the sick and injured, the homeless and the hungry. Help us to be good neighbours and to help others.
Amen.

The children could all remember one time when someone helped them, and then they could say thank you to God in turn for that person.

General theme

In what ways could we help someone lying injured in the street? In what ways can we be good neighbours?

Who do you think is our neighbour, in the way Jesus meant? Is it just those who live near to us?

How can we be good neighbours? How can we be good neighbours to people in other countries?

Christian theme

Does pleasing God mean just keeping the rules?

Michael wanted to know if Jesus was a bad man or a good man. What do you think he felt after hearing Jesus?

Why do you think Jesus used stories when he was teaching?

Extension ideas

1. Let the children think about helping others. They could list all the ways that they could help people. They could perhaps try to do a good turn every day. (For their safety it would be a good idea to point out that some actions are more appropriate for adults.)

2. Michael had a decision to make: was Jesus good or bad? Write a story about someone finding out whether someone is good or bad.

3. Make a poster encouraging people to be good neighbours; for example, don't let your dog foul the playground, don't drop litter, etc.

4. Think about crime and safety. How can we avoid being a victim of crime? Perhaps organise a visit by the local beat police officer.

Zacchaeus' story:

Caught up a tree

Reference: Luke 19:1-10

General theme: Putting things right.
Christian theme: Jesus helps Zacchaeus change his life.
Way in: Have you ever done something very silly? How would you feel if someone had found you doing it?
Introduction: Today's story is about a man called Zacchaeus, who is so keen to see Jesus that he does something silly.

Story

I'm used to people hating me, but laughing at me, that really hurt. I've never felt so silly, but, then again, if I hadn't done it, then Jesus would never have seen me.

Let me introduce myself. My name is Zacchaeus and I live in a town called Jericho. I have a very important job and it's made me very rich. But although I always liked having money, even though I had lots, I still wasn't happy.

You see I was rich because of my job, and it's a job a lot of people don't like. So they don't like me. I am a tax collector. I take money from people and give it to the government. Because the Romans have taken control of our land, the money I collect goes to them. So a lot of people call me a traitor.

Some tax men take too much money, they steal and cheat. People think I do too. So no one wants to talk to me or be my friend. I get very lonely, without friends.

One day a man called Jesus came through our town. He had become really famous round here and everyone went out to see him. I wanted to see him too.

But I had a problem: I'm very short. When I got to the road and joined the crowd waiting at the side, I couldn't see anything but the backs of people's heads. I so wanted to see Jesus, I didn't want to miss him. He talks to people like me, people nobody else wants to know.

I couldn't see, but I could hear people shouting. Jesus was coming and I was going to miss him. I looked around wildly for some way to see him, for a space in the crowd. I didn't want to

29

have to push and shove like the others; it's not very dignified for a man in my position.

Then I spotted the tree. It had a thick trunk and plenty of strong branches, and lots of leaves. I don't know what made me do it. It's not the sort of thing I usually do. But I thought, if I climb the tree and sit on one of the branches, I can see Jesus properly. So, without thinking, I kicked off my sandals and tucked up my robes and started to climb. I haven't climbed a tree since I was a boy, when I had friends to do things with. I made a bit of a mess of it at first, slithered about and grazed my knees. Then it all came back to me and I was getting higher and higher. I felt like a bird.

At first no one noticed me. Everyone was looking the other way to see Jesus. Anyway, I'm small and no one takes much notice of me. As I climbed I could see more and more. I could see over everyone's head. I was pleased no one could see me though: I'm an important man; I spend my life trying to be dignified, I didn't want to look silly.

It felt safe in the tree. I could see everyone, and they couldn't see me. I could see Jesus coming along the road with his friends. They were chatting and laughing.

When Jesus got to my tree, he stopped suddenly and looked up. He peered up through the leaves as though he was looking for something. I shrank as far back as I could get, trying to hide. But he saw me. He said, 'Zacchaeus, come down now. I'm coming to stay at your house today.'

I couldn't believe it. Everyone was looking up at me and laughing, making fun of me. I felt so foolish. What could I do? It was too late to hide. And I couldn't stay up in the tree for ever. Already one or two of the lads were shaking the tree, trying to shake me out.

And then, as I sat there panicking, I suddenly realised something. Jesus knew my name! Not only that, but he wanted to come to my house and eat with me! No one ever wanted to come to my house. Then, without thinking, I let go, and I came down that tree so fast. I slithered and bumped my way down, crashing through the branches. When I got to the bottom I must have looked a mess. Bits of twig were in my hair and leaves were sticking out of my clothes. Usually I would have been really embarrassed to be seen like that. But today I didn't care: Jesus was coming to my house.

I greeted Jesus and started to show him the way. I didn't know what I was saying. I was just so happy to be with him and his friends.

But people in the crowd began to complain. They said, 'Zacchaeus is a sinner, a bad man. Jesus can't go to his house.'

Jesus didn't say anything, but I was afraid he'd change his mind, that he wouldn't want to come. I'm not as bad as some tax collectors; but somehow, standing next to Jesus, I knew my best wasn't good enough.

I turned to those who were muttering, and I said, 'Lord, I have so much, I'll give half of everything I have to those that don't have enough. And if I've cheated anyone, I'll pay them back over and over to make up for it.'

I so wanted Jesus to come to my house. He looked at me then, and said things that I don't fully understand, but they made me feel good inside. He said that I was a son of Abraham, still part of the Jewish people, not a traitor after all. He said I'd been saved that day. I think that meant that God accepted me, even though I'd got things wrong. He said that he had come to look for and save what was lost. I suppose he meant me.

We went off together, as some people grumbled and others cheered. I don't care about the money. I've got something far more important. I've got Jesus coming to supper at my house.

I don't understand all that's happened. I'm going to have to think about it. But Jesus knows all about me and wants to be my friend. I may be a small man, but a big change has happened in my life.

Performance

The narrator could have piles of money in front of him or her to count. The story could be mimed or acted out, with children acting as the crowd, blocking the view and calling out as appropriate. It could also be told using finger puppets for the main characters.

Prayer

Dear God,
Thank you for friends. Thank you that you want to be our friend, even when we get things wrong. We pray for the lonely, that you will bless them and that they might find friends.
Amen.

The children could draw pictures of their friends. They could thank God for them by name and ask God to bless them.

General theme

What makes a good friend?
Zacchaeus wanted to put things right, and to give some money back. What things do we do wrong and how can we put them right?

Do you know what taxes are? (If not, explain.) Sometimes taxes can be used for good things like hospitals, etc. What would you use the money for?

Christian theme

People judged Zacchaeus without really knowing him – do we do this sometimes?

Zacchaeus learned that Jesus wanted to be his friend, even though he got things wrong sometimes. How do you think Zacchaeus would have felt and would it have changed him?

Extension ideas

1. Zacchaeus counted; the children could play counting games and play with or learn about money; younger children could have a play shop.
2. Do a painting, model or collage of trees or seasons, or make leaf prints.
3. Zacchaeus had to put things right, and give back some of the money he had stolen. Write a story about someone who has to return something to its rightful owner.
4. If appropriate go for a walk and count the different trees seen. The children could also do a project on the different types of trees – deciduous, evergreen, etc. – or on the cycle of the seasons.

Philip's story:

A stormy day

References: Mark 4:35-41; Matthew 8:23-27; Luke 8:22-25

General theme: Dealing with fear.
Christian theme: Jesus has power over the weather.
Way in: Have you ever been out in a storm? What was it like?
Introduction: This story is about Philip, who had a very scary day.

Story

Have you ever been really, really scared? I have. Let me tell you about it.

We'd had a good day, listening to Jesus teaching the crowds who were following us. He told them all sorts of stories, stories about gardening, farming and people. Silly stories, funny stories, sad stories. Each one had its own meaning. Sometimes when we didn't understand what they were all about, Jesus would explain them to us.

He'd been telling stories all day. When evening came he said to us, 'Let's go to the other side of the lake.' I was pleased because I thought we would get some peace at last. And we would have Jesus to ourselves. We'd had such a busy day we needed a rest; I guess Jesus felt the same.

We all clambered into a boat on the shore and sailed out into deep water. It was a beautiful evening and it was peaceful on the lake. The fishermen in our group got on with sailing, while I stayed with Jesus in the stern of the boat. We chatted and relaxed. The boat bobbed up and down. Gradually Jesus' eyes closed and he fell asleep, resting on a cushion. He was so tired.

I felt tired too, but I couldn't get to sleep. I tossed and turned on the hard wooden floor of the boat. Then when I finally got comfortable, with my cloak under my shoulders, the others started singing. I shouted at them to keep it down, but they just laughed. So, I stared out across the water, watching the waves and the other boats.

When we got into the boat, the sky had been clear blue, but now as I watched I could see dark clouds gradually building up on the horizon. I called over to a friend and pointed at the clouds. He said not to worry, we'd be across the lake before the storm came.

I wanted to believe him, but the clouds looked heavy and dark. They seemed to be racing across the sky. The air around us became chilly, and a wind sprang up. I drew my cloak around me. The wind tugged at our hair, it blew around Jesus. But still he slept.

I asked my friend what was happening. He said that a storm was coming, but not to worry. They often blew up on the lake, he said. The sky grew so dark it was almost black. The sun disappeared behind the clouds. The wind began to blow faster. The boat was tossed on the waves. It was difficult to stand up. Still Jesus slept.

Then lightning flashed across the sky. The thunder rumbled around us. The winds grew stronger, I thought the sails would break. Jesus slept on.

The fishermen were working hard to keep the boat on course, and upright. The rain lashed down, soaking us to the skin. The waves began to come into the boat. The boat rolled fiercely. Jesus slept.

Now we were calling out to one another in fear. Even the fishermen said that they had never seen a storm like this one. We began to think that we wouldn't make it to the other side. We were all trembling, but not with the cold. One or two began to pray. In all this noise and fear, a figure lay still, quietly sleeping in the stern. Jesus was unaware of the storm. How could he sleep when we were in danger of drowning in that cold, dark water?

Suddenly overcome by fear and anger, I called out, 'Teacher, we're going to drown. Don't you care?'

Jesus woke up. He stood up in the boat, in the middle of that fierce storm. He looked down at the waves and up into the sky, and he said, 'Be still. Quieten down.' The wind died down. The sea became calm. The waves vanished. Once more we were bobbing quietly in the water.

He looked around at us, sorrowfully, and said, 'Why were you so afraid? Don't you trust me?'

Now we were really terrified, but in a different way. Not with the kind of fear that makes your bones feel as if they're melting inside you. But with a deep wonder at what we had seen. We all whispered to one another, 'Who is Jesus? Even the wind and waves do what he tells them.'

Jesus could make a storm go away by speaking to it. He was stronger than the storm. We were amazed at his power, excited by what had happened, and thrilled that he cared for us.

Performance
This story could be done as a dramatic reading or action story, with sound effects for the storm and the children pretending to bale out the boat and lower the sails. A pretend boat could be made, using a blanket or arranging chairs to form the right shape.

Prayer
Dear God,
Thank you God for different kinds of weather, we know we need both sun and rain. Thank you for the world that you have created, and thank you for caring for us. Help us when we get frightened, and please help all those in dangerous situations. Amen.

The children could paint pictures of different kinds of weather, and then hold up their pictures while they thank God.

General theme
What makes us feel frightened? (This should be done sensitively.)
What makes us feel safe?
How can we cope with our fears? (Some things we should be frightened of, to keep safe, other fears stop us from living a full life.)
How do you think Jesus' friends felt afterwards?

Christian theme
Do you think God wants us to feel afraid?
What do you think that this story shows us about God? (He is powerful, and he cares for his creation.)
Why do you think Jesus was able to still the storm?

Extension ideas
1. Keep a weather chart for a few weeks.
2. The children could do a project on different sorts of weather. Younger children could look at different things needed for different kinds of weather – sun hats, boots, etc.
3. Make a weather mobile either with weather symbols or different sorts of clothes. Or make a windmill.
4. Write or read weather poems.

Nicodemus' story:

An adventure in the dark

Reference: John 3:1-21

General theme: Letting people have their say (free speech).
Christian theme: Jesus changes our ideas about God.
Way in: Have you ever had to do something really difficult, something you didn't want to do? What did you feel like?
Introduction: This story is about a man called Nicodemus. He was a Pharisee, that is, he was a religious teacher, and a member of the ruling council, which was called the Sanhedrin. He was chosen by the others to do something that no one else wanted to do.

Story

I was the one chosen. I drew the short straw, no doubt about it. Everyone wanted to know the answer, but no one wanted to be the one to go and find out. At best, it could be very embarrassing, and at worst it could be very, very dangerous.

Let me try to explain. All my life I've read the scriptures, our holy books, and tried to understand them and teach them to others. One thing I've learnt is that God is not something that you can put into a box. You can't say, that is God, that's what he's like. God is always surprising. Not because he changes his mind, but because we have such small minds. We can't understand his ways.

So when Jesus came along, preaching, healing and gathering followers, some of my friends on the Sanhedrin thought he was bad, and should be stopped. 'He's been taken over by a demon; he's working for the devil,' they said. 'He's challenging all that we understand about God.'

Well that last bit was true. He certainly said and did things that we found difficult. But I didn't believe he was bad. I wondered if maybe he was someone special sent from God.

We talked and thought and argued, and eventually someone said, 'We've got to go and find out more about him. So that we can judge if he's been sent from God or not.' We all agreed on that, but then came the question of who was going to go. It could be risky being seen with this troublemaker. Feelings were running high, you could even get yourself killed. It needed to be done in secret.

A meeting with Jesus was arranged. Don't ask me how, I don't know. It was all very hush-hush. The meeting was to be at night, somewhere quiet where no one could see. One of us would spend time alone with Jesus, and decide if following him was worth the risk.

I was chosen. That night as I waited, I felt both scared and excited. I'd get a chance to ask Jesus what he was all about, what he thought he was doing.

When the time came I was led down dark alleyways. When anyone came by, my guide would make me wait in the shadows. My heart began to pound. Everyone else was tucked up safe and sound at home, and here I was off to meet someone who could be a troublemaker or a madman.

Eventually, we came to a dark house, and I was ushered in to Jesus' presence. A small lamp was lit, and I could see Jesus' face softened by the shadows. It was very quiet in the room, and apart from my beating heart, very peaceful. Jesus looked tired. He led a hard life, always on the move, people always wanting him to do things. He waited for me to speak.

I said, 'Teacher, we know that you come from God, because of all the miracles that you do. Only God could help you do those things.'

And then I stopped. All the questions went out of my head. He was so still, so calm. And then he said something I couldn't understand. He said, 'You can't get into God's kingdom without being born again.'

Puzzled, I said, 'How can someone go back into their mother and be born again?'

Then he said, 'To get into God's kingdom you must be born of water and of the spirit. After all, flesh is flesh and spirit is spirit.'

I began to understand that he wasn't talking about our bodies being born again, but our spirits, our souls inside. John the Baptist baptised with water, and that was a new beginning, but Jesus meant something more than that.

He continued, 'God's spirit is like the wind: it goes where it wants, you can't keep it caged.'

I said, 'How does this happen?'

Jesus said to me, 'You're supposed to be a teacher, but you can't understand. I've tried to explain things simply for you because you can't understand heavenly things. Only I can because I come from heaven.'

He went on to say a lot more things and I just listened. He

talked about how God loved the world so much that he sent Jesus to us. He said that we could see whether people were bad or not by what they did.

The time I spent with him seemed to go really quickly. Just before the sun rose, I said thank you to him and slipped quietly away. The next day I met the others and told them all that Jesus had said. It started a big argument. Some left, feeling that Jesus was getting too big headed because he said that he was like God. Some of our group began to follow Jesus in secret. Some waited to see what would happen next before they made up their minds.

I thought that Jesus was letting God out of the box that we had tried to put him in. He said that we didn't know what God would do because we didn't know enough. Just as we couldn't tell where the wind comes from, or goes to. We've always thought that we could get to heaven by being good. Jesus said it's more complicated than that. We have to allow God's spirit to work. He's changing what we think we know about God, and that's uncomfortable. But suddenly God seems bigger than he did yesterday.

Performance

To create atmosphere the story could be read in the dark, by torch or lamp light. A mime could be done for part of the story, with the children pretending to creep through the streets at night without being seen.

Prayer

Dear God,
Please help us when we are frightened. Please help us when we have to do something difficult, or we have a hard choice to make. Give us wisdom to make right choices.
Amen.

The children could make up their own prayer, to a pattern like the one given. I get scared when I'm (in the dark/on my own), but I feel safe and strong when (the light is on/I'm with others). Thank you God for (light/other people). Amen.

General theme

Nicodemus and his friends had an argument. Do you ever argue with your friends? How do you sort things out when you argue? Some of Nicodemus' friends decided to follow Jesus, but kept it a secret. Do you think this was the best way? Why?

Jesus was challenging the way people thought about things and some wanted to stop him from talking. Are there some people whose ideas we find difficult to hear today? Is it a good idea to stop them from having their say?

Christian theme

Nicodemus thought that Jesus was letting God out of the box. Do we put God in a box? How? And how can we let him out? What do you think it might mean to be born again?

Jesus was saying that God wants more than people doing good things. Do we need to do good things if we believe in God? If we are 'born again' as Jesus said, does that mean we can do what we like?

Extension ideas

1. Write a story about a night-time adventure.
2. Make a collage of sunset or night time, with the outline of buildings against the sky and bright lights in houses, and the stars and moon.
3. Nicodemus was frightened that he would face reprisals for following Jesus. Discuss the importance of religious tolerance and freedom of speech. Look at how our country and others have faced this problem, in the past and today.
4. Some creatures only come out at night. Learn which animals come out at night and how they are adapted to this. Have pictures on the walls.

Joanna's story:

An unexpected healing

References: Mark 5:21-43; Matthew 9:18-26; Luke 8:40-56

General theme: Helping those who feel left out.
Christian theme: The power of faith.
Way in: Who has been ill? What does it feel like? What's the worst part?
Introduction: This story is about a woman called Joanna, who had been ill for a very long time.

Story It's so exciting, I must tell someone! I can't stop smiling and I may do a little dance in a minute. I must tell you what's happened to me. Jesus has changed my life. I thought I was going to be ill forever. I have been for 12 years, bleeding all that time, and where I come from that made people call me unclean.

I had to stay alone because if I touched anyone, that made them unclean too. Although my illness is painful, feeling left out of things has been worse. No one wants me near them. I can't join in the gossip that goes on by the well, and in the market place. I can't see people married. I can't hold my grandchildren and play with them. Sometimes people shout across to me to tell me something or to ask how I am, but no one ever comes close. I may touch them, even by accident, and make them unclean.

You may be wondering why I don't do something about it. Don't talk to me about doctors. I've tried doctors. I've walked miles to see them, and paid them so much money. They've given me disgusting things to drink, and other remedies I daren't even describe to you, but nothing has made any difference.

I've got used to going out when there is no one else about, either early in the morning before anyone's up, or I scuttle about in the dark, with the other creatures that frighten people.

I don't know what made me do it. If I'd known all that was going to happen I'm not sure I'd have been brave enough. Even though my life has changed. I'd heard about Jesus, of course, you can't live round here and not hear about him. I'd heard about his teaching and miracles. He heals people. Just like that. No money, no dreadful potions to take. Just a look or a word. Anyway, today curiosity got the better of me. I decided to go and see him, this holy man not afraid to talk to us outsiders. I thought, I'll just take a look at him, and maybe his goodness shining through will help me through the day. I covered myself up so no one would recognise me, and set out.

It was easy to find him. There was a big crowd round him. I joined them as they followed Jesus along the dusty roads, down the narrow lanes between the houses. He seemed to have time for everyone. He didn't hurry, even when one of the synagogue leaders asked Jesus to heal his daughter, who was very ill.

I passed the people he'd spoken to and I could see their faces shining with joy and hope. As I followed, I began to dream that he would speak to me and touch me and I would be well again. But it couldn't happen. He didn't know I was there, and I couldn't ask him now, when he had a sick girl to heal. Besides, if people saw me they'd turn me away; he's a holy man and I'm unclean.

But then I thought, perhaps I could just touch him without him knowing, and that would make me better. I had to try it.

I drew my robe closer round my head and began to move through the crowd, closer to Jesus. I was bumping against so many people, but they didn't recognise me. I hadn't been among so many people for a long time, and I'd forgotten the smell of hot, sticky bodies. I was in the crowd coming up behind Jesus. I was so close I could touch the fringed end of his cloak. He wouldn't know; no one would.

I reached out and touched his clothes. Immediately the bleeding stopped, and I felt well again. The pain went and I felt strong. I felt like dancing. I quietly began to draw back, to let the crowd pass by me again.

I knew I was well. I needed a moment to myself to think about it. To hug that knowledge to myself. But Jesus stopped. He looked around the crowd, and for one second our eyes met. He knew, I swear he did.

He said, 'Who touched my clothes?' That made people smile.

His friends said, 'Look at this crowd. How can you ask who touched you?'

But he knew. He stayed still, and as he looked in my direction, I knew I had to go and tell him. When he looked at me, I knew he knew more about me than any other person ever had.

I was so frightened, because I would have to own up in front of the whole crowd. I would have to tell everyone what I had done. My shame and humiliation would be public. The joy I had felt at being healed fell away. Maybe, because of what I had done, my illness would come back, or Jesus would tell me off.

I came forward in a rush, and threw myself at his feet. Somehow lying in the dust seemed the safest place to be. I couldn't be made any lower. I lay on the ground, my head pressed against the earth and told him what I had done. How I was healed when I touched his clothes.

The crowd gasped. I waited for Jesus to tell me off. I felt shame burning through me. Then Jesus spoke to me. He said, 'Daughter, you trusted in me and your faith has healed you. Go in peace.'

He called me daughter, this great and holy man! He was telling me I had done the right thing, that I hadn't done anything wrong by touching him. I hadn't realised until he spoke that the curiosity that I had earlier had been replaced by a deep trust and faith in Jesus. As I had seen him talking to people on the roads, I knew he could do anything and I knew he was someone I could trust. And now I could go in peace, because my faith in him had not been misplaced.

I looked up to thank him, but other people were talking to him. They were telling him that Jairus' daughter had died. I was scared again. Had a little girl died because I had stopped Jesus going to her. But Jesus said to Jairus, 'Don't be afraid. Just believe and she will be healed.'

He looked across at me as he said it, and I knew she would be healed. Just as I had been.

Performance

This would perhaps best be told plainly. This story could also be told using puppets for the main characters, or could be fully dramatised. Real or pretend doctor's or hospital equipment could be brought in – stethoscopes, thermometers, etc.

Prayer

Dear God,
Thank you for the times when we are healthy. Please help us when we are ill. Thank you for all those who look after us when we are ill: for family, doctors, nurses and all the others who care for us. We pray now for all those we know who are ill, and pray that you will bless them.
Amen.

Happy and sad faces could be used in the prayers. The children could make one of each and pick up the appropriate one when they say their prayer. Holding up a happy face when they thank God for something and a sad face when they ask God to bless someone who is ill.

General theme

Joanna didn't find the doctors very helpful. Doctors can do much more now. How can doctors help us? (for example, medicine, X-rays, operations, etc.)

How did Joanna feel when she was ill?

Are there people we know who might feel left out because of age, illness, language or culture? How can we make them feel part of things?

Christian theme

How do you think the people in the crowd might have felt about what happened to Joanna?

Why do you think Joanna trusted Jesus?

What does this story tell us about Jesus?

Extension ideas

1. A game such as 'Operation' could be played, where the children have to remove organs from a body. Or the children could explore a model of the human body, learning and naming its various parts.
2. The children could discuss and learn basic first aid, or practise bandaging.
3. The children could do a project on other countries where medical help is not so available, and agencies that help.
4. They might also do a picture or collage of a hospital scene, or of the woman after she was healed, with her friends.

Martha's story:

A busy evening

Reference: Luke 10:38-41

General theme: Learning when to stop.
Christian theme: Listening to God.
Way in: Have you ever had friends round for tea? What did you do?
Introduction: This story is about a woman named Martha, who had a very special guest.

Story   Sometimes it's the small things that can change your life in ways you don't expect. I mean later on we had more exciting moments in our family. Our brother Lazarus has a story to tell when you've got time. He came back from the dead; not many people can say that! But that was later when we knew Jesus better. My story goes back to when we'd just met Jesus.

Jesus was going from village to village, town to town, teaching anyone who would listen about God. Sometimes he had crowds of hundreds listening to him, sometimes he had a group of 20, and sometimes he would just be talking to one man and a goat. It didn't matter to Jesus. If someone wanted to hear about God, he would talk to them. He would tell stories and do wonderful things, like making blind people see. One day Jesus came to Bethany, our village, and we went to see him.

Bethany is a small village, very close to the big city of Jerusalem. It's right on the edge of the desert, on the slope of a mountain. So we have empty desert on one side, and the busy city of Jerusalem on the other. I think that's why Jesus liked coming here. He was near enough to Jerusalem to go to the Temple, but far enough away for him to get a bit of peace and quiet, when he'd had a long day.

I live with my younger sister, Mary. She's a bit of a dreamer. I'm always having to tell her to get on with things or nothing gets done. I suppose I nag her a little, but we get on most of the time. Our brother, Lazarus, lives in Bethany too.

Anyway, when Jesus came teaching in Bethany, I could see that he needed somewhere to stay. Somewhere he could put his feet up and have a meal. So I said to him, 'Teacher, you're welcome to come and eat with us.' And that's what he did.

I was pleased. It's not every day that a great teacher comes to our house. I wanted things to be really special for him. He was always looking after others, I thought he should have someone to look after him.

That's when things started to go wrong. The problem with inviting Jesus is that he doesn't come on his own. His disciples come too, and suddenly I had 13 extra hungry men to feed.

So the front room's full of men lying about on the straw mats on the floor, where they can reach the table. It's a good job it's a big airy room. I don't mean to be rude but they'd spent all day walking about in the sun, and they'd got hot and sweaty and a bit smelly.

I left them relaxing in the main room, after I'd got them wine and water to drink. I made sure they were comfortable and then left them to talk.

That's what we women do. We leave the men to talk over the big things in life and we get on with the cooking, cleaning and all the practical things. That's what used to happen, anyway.

I expected Mary to follow me into the courtyard to help me with the cooking. There were vegetables to prepare, bread to be baked and fruit to arrange. A lot of food and a lot of work. But she didn't come. She sat down at Jesus' feet and listened to him talk, as though she was one of the disciples.

So I had double the work to do. All those extra mouths to feed, and only my pair of hands to do it. I walked in and out, putting out dishes, serving out food, clearing it away and getting extra drinks. I banged and clattered, because I thought that Mary would notice and come and help me. But she didn't. She only sat and listened. Now I was the one getting hot and sweaty. And very cross.

I wanted to be part of it too. I started to listen to Jesus once or twice, but then I would smell the bread burning, or see the animals out in the yard getting too interested in our food. Out I'd rush flapping my arms and running around. When I got back Jesus would be talking about something else, and I'd have missed what he was saying.

Eventually, I got so cross with Mary, that I forgot that Jesus was a teacher, and our guest. I forgot to be polite. I marched over to Jesus and said, 'Don't you care that Mary is leaving me to do all the work. She's done nothing to make you comfortable. Tell her to come and help me.'

Jesus looked up at me, looking strangely sad, and said, 'Martha, Martha,' in such a gentle tone. 'You're worried about so many things. But only one thing is really needed. Mary's got the right idea. And no one's going to take that away from her.'

The gentleness in his tone, and the sad look in his eyes, made me realise that I'd got it wrong. The anger inside melted away as I looked at him, and thought about what he had said. And then I understood. I'd wanted to give something special to Jesus, but he had something even more special to give to me. No other teacher talked to and listened to women as equals. He was offering a gift to Mary and to me that no one else would. He was enabling us to hear about God first hand, from him. We didn't have to ask someone else what he'd said later. He was right, this was more important. I couldn't turn down that offer. The food could wait.

Performance

Have one child being Martha, running around busy all the time the story is being told, until the end when they sit down and listen.

Prayer

Dear God,
Thank you for people who look after us and prepare our meals. Thank you for things to do and thank you for quiet times too. Amen.

Each child could have a small bag, and they could call out in turn tasks that they have to do, such as cleaning teeth, homework, or cleaning out the gerbils. Each time someone mentions a task a weight is put in the sack. At the end in turn they say, 'Please God, help us with all we have to do', and the teacher or someone else lifts the heavy bag away.

General theme

Martha did not expect to listen to Jesus because she was a woman. Are there things that only men or women can do, or are we used to it being done one way?
Martha was too busy too listen or to think, why do you think Jesus said Mary had got it right?
When we are busy how can we relax?

Christian theme

Why didn't Jesus ask Mary to help Martha? Was Martha wrong?
God has told us (in the Ten Commandments) not to work all the time. Why do we need rest?
What does God want us to do with the free time?
What does this story show us about God? (He values each one of us and wants us to spend time with him.)

Extension ideas

1. Get the children to draw or write out their typical day, getting up, getting ready for school, homework, time with friends and time with family. They could chart out their day, marking off what is work and what is play/rest.

2. Get the children to collaborate in preparing a meal for a guest. What goes into getting it ready – working out a menu, shopping, cleaning, tidying, entertaining the guest?

3. Have the children write a story about a special guest or write about their sister/brother/friend who is very different to them, just as Mary and Martha were very different.

4. Arrange a quiet time or corner for the children where they can calm down and unwind. Use meditation, listening to music or stories. Get the children to talk about how it felt to have a quiet time afterwards – were they bored, sleepy, etc.?

Nathan's story:

A hard choice

Reference: Matthew 12:1-14

General theme: Listening to your conscience.

Christian theme: Following God's Law or man's law.

Way in: Have you ever seen someone doing something wrong? Is it easy to go against your friends if they ask you to join in stealing, bullying, etc.?

Introduction: This story is about a religious teacher called Nathan who had a difficult decision to make. His friends were going to do something very wrong and he didn't want to be part of it.

Story

You can't blame me for what happened later. I may have agreed on this day, I didn't have time to think it all over. It happened too quickly. But I did the right thing in the end. At least I think I did.

It all happened on one holy day, the Sabbath, Saturday. Moses had given us God's Law many years ago, and it said that we could work on six days. But the Sabbath day had to be kept free of work. The Sabbath was there for us to worship God. Many questions had been asked over the years about what was and wasn't work. Those of us who taught the Law had come up with a set of rules, which covered everything. We knew what people could and couldn't do on the Sabbath. Those who broke the rules would be punished. The punishment for lighting a fire was death.

Now we were watching Jesus. We were worried about him. He and his followers were stirring people up, getting them excited. People were beginning to listen to him and not us. Our Roman rulers were beginning to notice that something was happening. We liked it when it was nice and quiet, and people did what we told them.

On this Saturday we followed Jesus and his friends into a corn field. The field was planted in long strips, with a path running through it. According to our law it was all right to pick some ears of corn in the field if you were hungry. As long as you didn't take too many, it wasn't stealing. Jesus and his friends were hungry and they began to pick the ears of corn and eat them.

'Aha!' we said to Jesus, 'You've got it wrong. You and your disciples are breaking the Law. By picking the ears you are harvesting, and by rubbing the ears together you are preparing food. This is all work, and you've done it all on the Sabbath.'

Jesus didn't look guilty or worried. He said, 'Don't you remember that our great King David broke the Law, when he and his friends went into the Temple, and ate bread that could only be eaten by the priests? And our priests break the law every week by working in the Temple on the Sabbath. But you don't think David or the priests are guilty, do you?'

We couldn't believe our ears; was he saying that he was as great as the priests or David? That was bad enough, but he went further. He said, 'God wants you to worship him with all your heart and not only follow rules. If you understood this you wouldn't go about telling people they are guilty when they're not. After all, the special one sent from God is in charge of the Sabbath.'

So now he was telling us that we didn't know what we were doing. Even worse, it sounded as though he was saying that he was the special one sent by God!

He went on to the synagogue, the local place of worship. We followed on, talking and arguing as we went, trying to decide what to do. Had he gone mad, challenging us like that? Didn't he know how powerful we were?

In the synagogue there was a man whose hand was paralysed. Some of my friends now decided to try to trick Jesus into doing something really wrong. So they pointed out the man with the paralysed hand and said to Jesus, 'Is it wrong to heal someone on the Sabbath?'

We all knew that it was against the law unless someone was dying. This man wasn't dying; he'd been like it for years.

Jesus turned to us and said, 'I know what you're thinking. But if you had a sheep that fell down a hole on the Sabbath, I know you'd go down and get it out. And this man is more important than a sheep. So, yes, the Law does allow us to heal on the Sabbath.' He turned to the man who was looking a bit scared and confused, and said, 'Stretch out your arm.' And without thinking the man held out his hand and it was well again, just like his other hand.

Well, I stood there with my mouth open. I had seen someone who had been paralysed for a long time healed. This was a miracle. It was wonderful and Jesus had done it. Perhaps he was the Messiah, the special one sent from God.

My friends were furious with Jesus though. They felt that he had made them look stupid. They were worried that he was so clever that they couldn't trap him with questions. People were following him because he healed people. They wanted to stop him. They decided that the only way to stop him was to kill him. They quickly had it all sorted out, when and how they would kill him.

I was shocked. I didn't think that Jesus deserved to die. Not for making them look silly, not for healing someone. I thought and thought what I should do. Who was right? It made me feel sick thinking about it. There wasn't much time; it was going to be done soon, before he could stir up any more trouble.

I decided. I went and told Jesus all about the plot. I didn't wait for thanks. I betrayed my friends, because I wanted to save Jesus. I told Jesus, and he left and went somewhere else. I saved him then. I wish I could have done the same again later.

Performance

During the telling of the story, the group could be split into two. One half could be disciples and mime plucking ears of corn and eating them, following Jesus. The other half could be Pharisees, shaking their heads and wagging their fingers to show disapproval.

Prayer

Dear God,
Sometimes it's hard when our friends do something wrong and want us to join them. Please help us to make right choices.
Amen.

The children could make up a poem or rap to use as a prayer. It should be about the issues that bother them, such as stealing, lying, cheating, taking drugs or bullying. They could then perform it.

General theme

Nathan had a hard decision to make. Although he didn't like Jesus, he didn't want to see him killed. Have you had to make hard choices? What would you do if you knew a friend was going to do something wrong?
How do we know what things are right and what things are wrong?
In today's story, a good law, having a rest on the Sabbath, had been made so complicated that it was practically impossible to keep. Can you think of any examples of laws or rules which have got too complicated? (For example, some school uniform rules, parking regulations.)

Christian theme
Why were the Pharisees, the religious leaders, cross about what Jesus had said?

Do you think that when God said to rest on the Sabbath, that he had in mind all that the Pharisees had added? What do you think God meant?

What does this story tell us about Jesus?

Extension ideas
1. Draw up a rule book for behaviour in the classroom. See what rules can generally be agreed on.
2. Write a story about a plot that was foiled.
3. The Pharisees were angry. Paint a picture about what makes you angry.
4. Have a drama workshop on acting on your conscience. Think about people who have done so: conscientious objectors to war, Greenpeace, people who hid Jews in the Second World War. What was wrong? What motivated them? Did anything change? After the discussion, through the workshop, create and perform a play.

Rebecca's story:
A surprise at the well

Reference: John 4:1-42

General theme: Sharing good things.

Christian theme: Jesus changes an outcast into a celebrity.

Way in: If something really exciting happened to you, what would you do? (Tell my friends.)

Introduction: This story is about a woman called Rebecca, who had her life changed when she least expected it.

Story

It was a long hot walk to the well. It's way outside the village of Sychar, where I live. But I need the water, so I've got to go there. It's lonely too. The other women get their water nearer the village, but they don't like me and they show it. I've had too many husbands for their liking. Perhaps they think I'm bad luck, or a bad influence.

So I come here, where no one comes. I come at times of the day when it'll be quieter, so I don't see the others staring and pointing. I think a lot on my walk. Well I don't get much chance to gossip, do I? All the gossip's probably about me anyway. Or rather it was.

I was surprised to see him sitting at the well. He looked very tired and his eyes were closed. I remembered the group of men I'd passed on the way. They must be his friends. I'd kept out of their way. But I'd noticed them all right, chatting and joking. I guess they'd gone to get food from the village. So he was on his own like me.

And then he spoke to me. That was the second surprise. I mean, I'm a woman and a Samaritan, and he's a man and a Jew. Two good reasons not to talk to me. He said, 'Could you give me a drink?'

I said to him straight, 'Why are you, a Jew, asking me, a Samaritan woman, for a drink?'

He smiled and said, 'If you knew who it was who was asking you for a drink, you'd be asking me instead, and I'd give you living water.'

Well, I was beginning to think that he'd gone a little crazy from sitting in the hot sun. I said, 'How can you give me water? You haven't got a bucket, and the well is deep. Or are you cleverer than our ancestor, Jacob, who found this well. Are you going to find a running stream in this barren land?'

He didn't seem to mind my rudeness. He looked down at the well, and said, 'Anyone who takes a drink from this well will get thirsty again. But anyone who takes a drink from the water that I can give them, they will never be thirsty again. And they will live forever.'

He didn't seem crazy, but his words were strange. I thought, either he is mad, or he really can do what he says. Maybe he's a magician. So because I was curious, I said, 'OK then, give me some of this water of yours, so that I don't get thirsty again, or have to come all this way with my bucket to get water.'

I waited, thinking, that'll show you, making fun of me when I'm tired and hot. But when he spoke again, he said something completely different. 'Go and call your husband and tell him to come here.'

That caught me by surprise and I was a bit embarrassed. So I just said, 'I don't have a husband.'

He looked at me then, I mean really looked, like he could see right through me. He said, 'Well done. You're right to say that you don't have a husband. You've had five husbands, but the man you're with at the moment isn't your husband. You're speaking the truth.'

I was shocked. How could this stranger know so much about me? Only one way I could think of. He must be a prophet sent from God. I said, 'I can see you're a prophet sent from God. So can you tell me where we should worship God? Is it here as we believe, or in Jerusalem as the Jews believe?'

He said, 'It doesn't matter to God where you worship. It's *how* you worship that's important. One day people will worship God truthfully, as he wants.'

I'd never had a conversation like this before. He talked like no one else. I said, 'I know someone special, the Messiah, will come one day, and he will show us everything.'

This man in front of me said, 'I am speaking to you, and I am he.'

Well, before I had a chance to answer or think about all of this, his friends came back. They didn't interrupt us, but they were surprised to see us talking. I could tell by the looks on their faces.

I left my water jar there and ran all the way back to the village, forgetting how hot it was.

I shouted to everyone, 'Come and see this man that knows everything about me. Can he be the Messiah?' They knew of course that a stranger was around, because his friends had bought food. But even so I must have looked as though something special had happened, because people usually ignore me. Now they ran and listened, and some said that he must be the Messiah when they heard what had happened.

A great crowd of us went back to this man, Jesus. We begged him to stay with us and teach us. He said yes, and he stayed with us for two days. Lots more people came to believe that he was the Messiah. They said, 'It's not just because of what you said that we believe. We've heard him now for ourselves, and we believe he is the Saviour of the world.'

He's turned my life upside down. I believe in Jesus as the Messiah, God's special one, and I'm not shunned by everyone anymore. I've got friends among the others who believe in Jesus.

Performance

This could be done as a drama, with people being given parts to speak. Space could be used for the villagers to run to Jesus if appropriate.

Prayer

Dear God,
Thank you for exciting times like [whatever is seasonally appropriate] when we are happy and excited. Help us to share our joy with others.
Amen.

Each child could share something good that has happened to them (a visit to the cinema, a birthday, etc.) and then say, 'Thank you God'.

General theme

Something exciting happened to Rebecca and she wanted to share it. Has anything exciting happened to you that you wanted to share with your friends? And even with those who don't like you? Rebecca found in Jesus someone she could follow. What do you think makes a good leader/role model/teacher?
Jesus surprised Rebecca by talking to her because she was a Samaritan and a woman. Are there people today who would be surprised if Jesus talked to them?

Christian theme

The Samaritans and the Jews had very different ideas about where and how God should be worshipped. Jesus said something different, that God wants truthful worship. What do you think he meant by that?

What would the difference have been to a) Rebecca and b) her community if she'd kept her meeting with Jesus to herself?
Why do you think Jesus talked to her?

Extension ideas

1. Try making a newspaper with the class, containing only good news.
2. Do an experiment, measuring how much water a plant uses in a day. Does it use more on hot days? Draw a graph or chart.
3. Make a model of a well. Or paint a picture of Jesus and Rebecca at the well.
4. The children could do a project on water. The importance of water, the uses to which we put it and the various ways we can obtain it (direct from a stream, from wells in the ground, by collecting rainwater, using dams, reservoirs, etc.).

Ben's story:

The triumphal entry

References: Matthew 21:1-11; Mark 11:1-11; Luke 19:28-40; John 12:12-19

General theme: Sadness in happy times.
Christian theme: Jesus is acclaimed by the crowd as king.
Way in: Have you ever been to a football match when your side is winning, or some other exciting event? What did it feel like being part of it?
Introduction: This story is about a boy called Ben, who had a very exciting day.

Story

It was like the biggest party ever. I'd never seen so many people. It was time to get ready for Passover. That's a huge celebration in spring. It's a time when we remember that God saved our great, great, ever-so-many great, grandparents from being slaves in Egypt.

Jerusalem's always busy, but at Passover it's like an ants' nest, with people everywhere. I live just outside Jerusalem, and often go into the city, but Passover is special. Many people come from far away, all talking in different languages. There are stalls selling all sorts of things and everyone's happy, and no one tells us children off.

Mum and Dad were going into Jerusalem because everyone was saying that Jesus was going that day. Everyone wanted to see him. They were saying that he'd brought a man, called Lazarus, back to life when he'd been dead for over four days. So people thought that he would do something exciting in the city, maybe even in the Temple itself.

We met up with Jesus' group, at a village just outside Jerusalem. Earlier he'd sent two of his followers off to get a donkey. As we arrived they were just bringing the animal back to Jesus.

Quite a large crowd had gathered around him. There were a lot of other children there, and we wriggled our way to the front so that we could see everything. Jesus never minds children round him, not like some of the other religious teachers.

Anyway, when the donkey arrived some folk took off their cloaks and spread them over the donkey's back. They made a kind of seat. I was close enough to feel its rough, grey hair and its warm breath on my arm. Then some people caught hold of Jesus and lifted him up onto the donkey's back. He looked like a king up there – except I think kings usually ride on horses.

When Jesus was settled comfortably, we set off on the dusty road to Jerusalem. Everyone was singing and shouting, and more people joined us on the way. By the time we got to the gate at Jerusalem, people were running up to see who was making such a noise and why.

'Who is it?' they shouted. 'Who is causing all this fuss?'

We would all shout back, 'It's Jesus, the prophet from Galilee.'

I felt I'd never been as happy as I was as we walked along together. I felt so important being close to Jesus. People were getting very excited and they began to throw their cloaks down on the road in front of Jesus and the donkey. Those that didn't have cloaks reached up and cut down branches, big palm leaves, and threw them down instead. The road began to look like a multicoloured blanket.

'Why's he so important?' people asked. And a chorus of other voices answered, 'He healed my brother'; 'He fed 5000 people'; 'He told me what God is really like'; 'He does things no one else can'; 'He's been sent by God'. It was so noisy, everyone was shouting and talking at once, questions and answers, and people singing songs on top of all the commotion.

Jesus rode on. We walked and ran and skipped and jumped beside him. We entered Jerusalem through the tall gates, and went on through the narrow streets, past the busy markets smelling of food, and hung with special Passover gifts. More people joined the throng, and the singing grew louder. The crowd were singing praises to God. And they sang about Jesus. They sang, 'God bless the king. He comes in God's name. God bless Jesus our king.'

There was so much colour and noise. It was so exciting. I joined in singing, 'Hosanna! God bless Jesus!' I looked up at Jesus, expecting him to be smiling and excited, as I was. But he looked sad.

We could see the Temple now, with its walls gleaming like snow, towering above us like mountains. Some of it was covered in gleaming gold. It looked like something from another world. It was so big that all the people climbing the stairs to the top looked like ants on an ant heap.

We were still all singing. Some people were singing in different languages to mine, because they'd come from a long way to be here for the Passover. No one had ever been welcomed like this.

'Jesus is king!' The song echoed round the walls of the Temple.

Some of the Pharisees, who'd come along to see what was going on, got angry. 'Teacher, tell them to shut up,' they said. There were Roman soldiers everywhere. Perhaps the Pharisees were worried that the Romans would start arresting people for treason, for shouting that Jesus was king when the Roman Emperor is in charge of everything. Jesus looked at them and said, 'If I told them to be quiet, the stones themselves would start to sing.' They went away, muttering to themselves.

I glanced up at Jesus and was surprised to see that he'd started to cry. All these people singing his praises, loving him, and there were big tears rolling down his face. He was crying over Jerusalem and the people in it. He said, quietly, 'Jerusalem, if only you realised that now is the time God has come to save you. But you don't understand, you can't see. And Jerusalem will be destroyed, not a stone will be left.'

The party went on, and I was still excited and singing, but now there was also a chill inside me, like something terrible was about to happen.

Performance

The children could act out the procession, dropping clothes and paper leaves before someone pretending to be Jesus. They could learn a praise song to sing as they walk around.

Prayer

Dear God,
Thank you for fun days and holidays, for days when we can run and jump and sing. Please help those who feel sad when others around are happy.
Amen.

The children could create their own praise song to God, or learn one to sing as a prayer.

General theme

The crowd thought Jesus was important. How do we show people that we think that they are important?
Jesus was sad when everyone around was happy. Has this happened to you or someone you know? What do you think it felt like? How could you help someone who felt like this?
Why do you think that the Pharisees wanted the crowd to be quiet?

Christian theme

Why were the people praising Jesus? What did they think of him? Why did the crowd think Jesus was a king? What do you think they expected him to do?

Jesus said that the people didn't understand. What do you think he meant?

If Jesus were here today, do you think people would praise him and treat him as important? Why or why not?

Extension ideas

1. Make and sing music fit for a king and have a procession.
2. Paint, or make a collage, of a king or queen in royal robes.
3. Do a project on transport. In Jesus' day important people rode on animals while others walked. What other methods of transport are there? Cars, boats, planes, trains, buses, carriages – get the children to bring in toys, models and pictures and make a display.
4. Write a story/poem about a king or queen or other royal person.

Daniel's story:

Jesus in the Temple

References: John 2:13-21; Matthew 21:12-13; Mark 11:15-17; Luke 19:45-46

General theme: Don't do that here!

Christian theme: Jesus challenges accepted Temple practice.

Way in: Have you ever been really cross when you saw someone doing something you thought was wrong? What did you do?

Introduction: This story is about a man called Daniel, whose job was to change money in the Temple.

Story

I don't know about prophet. The man's gone mad. Jesus his name is, and the sooner they get rid of him the better.

I'd been looking forward to Passover. Not 'cause I'm religious. I leave all that to the priests, and those with time on their hands. I've got a wife and children to feed. I don't have time for all that praying and listening to the scriptures that they go in for. Maybe one day, when I've got time.

No, I like Passover because of the crowds. It's such a big festival see, and they come from all over – all over the world, I reckon. It's good business, isn't it? They all come to the Temple, I mean that's the whole point of the pilgrimage, isn't it – to see God's house? And people mean money, that's what I always say.

The Temple authorities are happy to have us there. Well, we're part of it, aren't we? They need us. The priests have to have animals for the sacrifice – pigeons, sheep and cattle – so somebody has to sell them. And people need to buy them, and if they don't have Temple shekels, we can change their money for them. It's been done for years. We're as much part of the Temple as the priests or the cleaners.

And if we make a little extra on the side, where's the harm in that? It's market forces isn't it? The people need to buy and so we charge them what seems fair to us. Some may argue and say it's unfair, but they all pay up in the end. Where else are they going to go?

We'd heard Jesus arrive in town the day before. You couldn't miss him, the noise the crowd were making. They were shouting, 'God bless the king.' Well, the Temple authorities didn't like that.

They don't want anyone pretending to be the king. They're very comfortable with Herod and the Roman governors.

Anyway, the next morning he was back again with his crowd. I was sitting in the shade, under the pillars. I'd got my table all set out, with all the shekels that people would need. All in piles, already counted. You don't want to hold people up on such a busy day.

Well, I don't know what started it. I was busy with my customers. But even over the noise of all the people, I heard him shouting. He was shouting at my friend, Isaac, who had the pigeon stall next to me.

Jesus shouted out, 'This Temple is supposed to be a house for praying in. But you have turned it into a house for thieves with all your stealing! This should be somewhere to worship God, but you've turned it into a market place!'

Then, before Isaac knew what was happening, Jesus turned him off his stool. Threw him off his seat. Well, the pigeons squawked a bit, but they were unharmed. Isaac was terrified though. Then Jesus turned to me. 'You as well,' he said and I jumped up and ran. He turned my table right over. The money went everywhere. You could hear it clattering down all over the floor, as it rolled away under people's feet. I lost a fortune that day. I couldn't find half of the money again.

Isaac and I were cowering against a wall by now, but Jesus left us alone. He hadn't finished. Oh, no. He'd picked up a rope from somewhere, and he began waving it around like it was a whip or something. He frightened the sheep and the cattle, and he began to drive them all out of the Temple. It was chaos. Animals everywhere, people trying to get out of their way. The people round me were scrabbling for my money. I was too shocked to do anything.

Then Jesus blocked the way into the courtyards, shouting at everyone that the Temple was for prayer, not shopping. He looked so angry.

We get lots of teachers talking to groups of their followers in the Temple courtyards; we get beggars and all sorts, but I've never seen anything like this.

Well, the authorities got angry too. They marched over to Jesus in a flurry, and said, 'What right have you to do all this? We've allowed it. Can you do one of your famous miracles to show us that you have an authority greater than ours?'

Jesus said, 'If you tear down this Temple, I will build it up again in three days.'

They laughed themselves silly then. 'Three days!' they said. 'It took hundreds of workers 46 years to build it. Three days! Don't make us laugh.'

Jesus left then, without saying anything else. He didn't cause any more fuss. We complained to the authorities about all our lost income. We said that something had to be done. They let him come back again later and teach. I think they were frightened of the people. You see that was the strange thing. When he went mad and threw everything around, the people thought that he was God's messenger.

Performance   The children could add sound effect noises as appropriate: crowds, animals, money falling, etc.

Prayer   Dear God,
Help us to treat places of worship with respect. We pray that you will bless all those who work in churches, and help them keep the churches clean and beautiful. May your churches be places of peace and prayer.
Amen.

The children could learn that there is more than one way to pray. Various attitudes of praying could be used while they said a pray they know, like the Lord's Prayer. They could stand, with their arms raised or by their sides; they could sit or kneel, with hands together or loose on their laps; they could even try praying while prostrate. The idea is to show that all these ways are acceptable to God. He is interested in how people's attitudes are inside.

General theme   Why was Jesus angry? Because they were selling in the Temple or because they were stealing?
Jesus was angry because he could see something he thought was wrong. What things do you think would make you angry?
Jesus was saying that what was being done in the Temple was not appropriate for a place of worship. Can you think of some behaviours that are OK in one setting, but not in another? (For example, roller skating in the cinema.) Are there some sorts of behaviour, such as spitting, that are never acceptable in public?

Christian theme   Jesus had a particular view on what the Temple was for. What do you think church is for?
Jesus said the Temple should be a house of prayer. What can we pray about?
Can we pray outside of churches and other holy places? If so, why do we pray in churches?

Extension ideas

1. Visit your local church to find out what goes on there. What is considered sacred space in the church? What is and is not allowed in church?

2. Either find out what the Temple looked like and get the children to make a model, or make a model of your nearest church/cathedral.

3. Write a story on someone taking action when they see something wrong. Include any consequences to their actions.

4. The children could do a project on pressure groups and lobbies. People trying to correct injustice, such as Greenpeace, Amnesty International, the Jubilee Campaign against debt, the history of civil rights in America, or the anti-apartheid movement. Get the children to think about what they think is worth lobbying for; is there a pressure group for that?

Caiaphas' story:

The plot against Jesus

References: Matthew 26:1-5; Mark 14:1-2; Luke 22:1-2; John 11:45-53

General theme: Does the end justify the means?

Christian theme: The religious leaders plot to kill Jesus.

Way in: Sometimes it's tempting to do something wrong, if you think doing it will make something else right, such as lying to get out of trouble. Are some things always wrong?

Introduction: This is the story of a man named Caiaphas, who was the High Priest in charge of the Temple. He was a worried man.

Story Something has to be done about Jesus. And I suppose I'll be the one to do it. They all look to me because I'm High Priest. The decision-making all falls on me.

He couldn't carry on, not like that. Once he'd set the Temple in an uproar, it was too much. He may be a popular teacher, but there have been other teachers before him, and there'll be other teachers after him. What's so special about Jesus?

He's causing too much trouble. He's coming to the attention of the Romans. They don't like it when the people get excited about leaders. It might lead to a revolt, they might fight the Romans. If the Roman authorities thought that that was likely, they'd come in even greater force, and perhaps destroy the Temple, maybe the whole nation.

I called a meeting of the chief priests and the elders, at my palace, to discuss it. The problem of Jesus and what to do about him. He'd allowed the crowds to call him 'king' and 'King David's son'. He'd upset business in the Temple by driving out the traders. And he'd been telling the people that the priests no longer taught God's word. He'd actually called us sinners and hypocrites. We'd tried tricking him to make him look foolish so that people would stop following him. But that didn't work. He's too clever. We'd tried asking him to keep the crowds quiet, but he wouldn't listen.

If we can't stop him one way, we'll have to get rid of him another. Jesus has to die. That's what I told the others. It's better to let one man, Jesus, die, than to have the Romans destroy the entire nation. They don't care how many die, as long as they keep control.

So, Jesus must die, and soon. But how to do it? There's always so many of his followers around. If we try to kill him or arrest him in public, there'll be a riot. And the Romans will come running, just what we are trying to avoid. We need to do it secretly. That's what I told the others.

We gave orders that if anyone knew where Jesus was, they should come and tell us, so that we could arrest him. Then we could kill him. So we know where he is most of the time now. Not that he makes a secret of it, standing in the Temple preaching, bold as brass, when he knows we're out to kill him. What does it take to make him shut up?

We got the information about Jesus all right, but he was always with the crowds. Too dangerous to do anything. Then just as we wondered what to do, along comes this man, Judas, and offers him to us! He's one of Jesus' followers. A close friend, one of his trusted inner circle. Always with him. He came to us and said, 'I'll tell you where to find him when there's no one around.'

We questioned him, of course, to make sure he was serious. He said he would deliver Jesus to us, in the dark, in secret, with only his closest friends around. He'll use a special sign to show the soldiers who to arrest. He'll greet him and give him a friend's kiss, and the kiss will be the sign.

I don't know why this man, Judas, has decided to betray Jesus. Why would someone so close to Jesus decide to turn him in? We've offered him money, thirty silver coins. He'll take the money, but I don't think money's the reason he's doing it. I think he feels betrayed by Jesus. Jesus isn't who or what he expected. That's the idea I get anyway.

Odd that he feels betrayed by Jesus.

So now we just wait for the right moment, and the signal, and Jesus will be history.

Performance
This is best told very simply. It is a man deciding to have someone killed. He could count out the money very slowly and put it in a bag ready for Judas.

Prayer
Dear God,
We pray for the leaders in the world, who have to make hard decisions. Please help them to make good choices.
Amen.

Let the children make up their own prayer, along the lines of 'Dear God, Help us to (be kind/tell the truth) and not (upset people/lie), etc.' Let them write down their own good/bad choices and read them out.

General theme

What do we expect our leaders to do?

Was Caiaphas right? Why did he think he was?

Jesus was betrayed by his friend. How do you think Judas felt? How do you think Jesus felt when he found out?

Are some things always wrong, no matter what the consequences? For example, if the secret police knocked on your door and asked where your friend was, and you knew, would you lie, or tell the truth and betray your friend?

Christian theme

Caiaphas felt he was God's chosen leader as High Priest, and Jesus would not do as he was told. How could Caiaphas have known who was really doing God's will? (Bible, seeing Jesus' miracles as evidence, etc.)

How can we know what God wants us to do?

What are the qualities of Caiaphas' leadership, and Jesus' leadership? How are they similar and how are they different?

Extension ideas

1. Have a drama workshop. Work on a play where someone has a hard choice to make or someone is betrayed. Get the children to think how it might feel to be the betrayer or the betrayed, or someone who has to make a decision like Caiaphas.
2. Hold a mock election for a leader, whether for a classroom leader or for a world politician. What qualities make a good leader? How do you persuade someone to vote for you?
3. Write a story about betrayal or someone letting a friend down.
4. Use precious metals and stones as the basis of a project. Where are they found? How are they mined? How do they look before they are cleaned up? etc. Or the children could decorate a mirror or paper with shiny mosaics, glass beads or silver and shiny paper shapes to represent metals and jewels.

John's story:

The Last Supper

References: Matthew 26:17-30; Mark 14:12-26; Luke 22:7-14, 21-23; John 13:21-30

General theme: Looking after each other.
Christian theme: Jesus the leader becomes the servant.
Way in: Jesus wanted to have a special meal with his friends. What do you like doing with your friends?
Introduction: This story is told by a man called John, who was one of Jesus' 12 special friends.

Story   We'd had the most exciting week ever. We'd come to Jerusalem for Passover, with Jesus. The crowds had cheered and waved and sung as Jesus entered Jerusalem. Jesus had taught hundreds of people in the Temple each day, and even after he'd got angry and upset the money-changers, they still left him alone.

Things were really beginning to happen and everyone was talking about Jesus, and what he would do next. We never knew, so life was always a surprise. Now we were sharing a meal together in a large upper room. Jesus and his 12 closest friends. All had been prepared for our special celebration meal for Passover.

At first it just seemed like a normal evening. Jesus said, 'I've been so looking forward to sharing this meal with all of you.' But then soon after that he started saying strange things, saying that soon he would have to suffer. We didn't understand what that meant. What was he going to have to suffer? We loved him, we didn't want to think of him in pain.

But then as quick as he'd started talking about this, he changed the subject, and no one asked him what he meant. He took off his outer robe, and tied a towel round his waist. He filled a basin with water, and knelt down and began to wash our feet, as though he was a servant. Jesus washed our feet with water, and then dried them with the towel.

Well the first few of us had our feet washed before we knew what was going on. But we were shocked, this was a servant's job, and Jesus who was our leader was doing it. We should have been washing his feet. When Jesus got to Peter, Peter said, 'Are you going to wash my feet, Lord?'

Jesus said, 'You don't understand this now, but you will later.'

Peter curled his feet up out of the way. He was shocked and he said, 'No, you won't ever wash my feet.'

But Jesus said, 'If I can't wash your feet, you can't be my follower.'

So Peter had one of his sudden changes of heart, and he thrust his feet at Jesus, saying, 'In that case, Lord, don't stop at my feet, wash my head and my hands as well.'

I started to smile. Peter never did things by halves; he is definitely an all or nothing sort of person. Jesus smiled too at this and said, 'Peter, you only need your feet washed; the rest of you is clean. But it's not only cleanliness I'm talking about here, but being good. There is someone here tonight who is far from clean.'

We didn't understand what he meant, but we were afraid to ask. This meal was turning decidedly weird. First Jesus talks about suffering, then he washes feet like a servant, and now he's saying one of us is dodgy. I was beginning to feel a bit on edge. What was going to come next?

When Jesus had finished, he took off the towel, put on his robe and sat down at the table. He said, 'I'm not sure you understand what just happened. You call me Lord and teacher, which is right, but I've just done a servant's job. I've set an example for you to follow: you should wash each other's feet. Look after each other. None of you is greater than me and I've allowed myself to be humbled for you. I hope you can do the same for each other.'

Then suddenly Jesus got very upset. He looked near to tears. He looked round at us all, and said, 'One of you is going to betray me.'

We all looked at one another, trying to work out what he meant. I was sitting next to Jesus. Peter beckoned to me, I leant over and he whispered to me, 'Ask him who he means.'

So I moved closer to Jesus and whispered to him, 'Who is it, Lord?'

He said, 'I'll dip some bread into the sauce and give it to him.'

Jesus picked up a piece of bread, dipped it and gave it to Judas. Judas took the piece of bread, and Jesus said to him, 'What you have to do, do it quickly.' That's all. Judas got up quickly and left us. He hurried into the night, still carrying his bread with him.

I didn't say anything to the others. I just sat there feeling sad and confused. What was going on? Because Judas always carried the money, and they hadn't heard what Jesus said, the others thought he'd gone to buy something that we'd forgotten. I wonder if we would have stopped him, if we had known what was going to happen.

Jesus said a lot more that night, but those were the things that I remember most. Telling us not to be proud, but to look after one another's needs. And knowing that he was going to have to suffer and that Judas would betray him.

As the meal went on, he told us to drink wine, and eat bread to remember him. We didn't understand; we thought we would have him for years to come. He was still a young man. The memories I have of that night are bittersweet. Just like the food we eat at Passover to remind us of our escape from slavery in Egypt. We were so close to him, and he enjoyed being with us. But it was all about to change, forever.

Performance

This story could be told with everyone sitting round a table, as at the Last Supper. Someone could act out the washing of feet and the blessing and breaking of bread as the story is told.

Prayer

Dear God,
Help us not to be too proud to look after one another. Thank you for all those who look after us, and bless them.
Amen.

Serve one another in prayer. Pass the peace as in Holy Communion, or wash each other's hands in turn, saying, 'God, bless you.'

General theme

This was a special meal for Jesus and his friends, as they were celebrating Passover. How do you celebrate special times, Christmas or other religious festivals with your family and friends?
Jesus was their leader, but he did the job of a servant. Why?
Jesus wanted his friends to look after each other. In what ways can we help our friends and look after each other?

Christian theme

Jesus knew he would have to suffer and leave his friends. How do you think he felt?
Jesus asked his friends to eat bread and drink wine to remember him. Is this done now? When and why?
What does this story tell us about Jesus? Why do you think Jesus let Judas go?

Extension ideas

1. Bake bread together. Discuss how it is made and where the ingredients come from.

2. Get someone, perhaps a vicar, to explain Holy Communion (or the Lord's Supper, Mass, Eucharist – whatever the most familiar name is). How is it done and what are the various parts of the service?

3. Spend some time thinking how you could help each other and the wider community. Put some ideas into practice: picking up litter, weeding the school garden, etc.

4. Paint a picture or make a collage of Jesus at supper with his friends. Look at how artists have treated this subject in the past.

Simon of Cyrene's story:

Jesus' arrest, trial and death

References: Matthew 26:36-54; Mark 14:43–15:41; Luke 22:39–23:49; John 18:1–19:37

General theme: Coping with sad times.
Christian theme: Jesus the leader is killed.
Way in: Have you ever had to do something for someone when you didn't want to, like showing a new child round the school? How did you feel about it?
Introduction: Today's story is about a man called Simon. He was visiting Jerusalem for the holidays and he was made to do something that he didn't want to do.

Story

I'm here at the end. I'm glad I helped him, even if it was only in a small way. Not that I wanted to do it at the time, but when Roman soldiers grab hold of you and tell you to do something, you don't argue.

I found out the rest of the story later from Jesus' friends. I didn't know what was going on when I was pulled out of the crowd by the soldiers, and forced to carry this two-metre piece of wood.

I'd come up to Jerusalem from the country for the festival. I was walking along when suddenly there was all this noise around me. Roman guards were shouting, banging their swords against their shields and shoving people out of the way. And what for? A sorry sight of a man beaten, bleeding and staggering under the weight of this huge bit of wood. We all knew what it meant. Crucifixion. He was on his way to his death.

Some of the people around were crying – friends of his I supposed – others were looking away as if his fate was contagious, like an illness; some were mocking him and laughing at him.

He staggered and fell. That was when the soldiers grabbed me, and said, 'Here you carry it for him.' They pushed me forward. I picked up the heavy piece of wood and followed behind him.

We walked slowly on. Once when he heard some women crying, this man turned to them and said, 'Don't cry for me, weep for yourselves. Because if they do this to me, no one is safe.'

When we got to the bare hill outside Jerusalem, the soldiers stripped him, knocked him down to the ground and nailed him to the cross. There were two other wretches on crosses too. It was nine in the morning.

I couldn't leave, because he couldn't. I'd carried his cross, and now they lifted him high in the air, arms outstretched, helpless as a babe. I felt I just couldn't walk away, so I stayed.

He didn't curse or spit or scream. It was noisy there on that dusty hill of death. Friends of the condemned wailed and cried. The mob jeered and laughed. The soldiers chatted. I heard the rest of the story then, whispered by his friends to one another at the bottom of the cross, as the heat of the day grew stronger.

After supper with his friends, he'd gone into an olive grove to pray with some of them. They'd fallen asleep and he'd been left alone. Then one of his friends, Judas, who'd left earlier, returned and kissed him in greeting. Instantly a band of soldiers came up and arrested him. He had been betrayed. He'd spent that long, lonely night being hauled before the Jewish authorities, the Roman governor and Herod the king. He'd walked from place to place, being mocked and whipped in between. He'd been accused of all sorts of things. There was no evidence, of course, but when did that ever matter?

Pilate, the Roman governor, had tried to release Jesus as a special gift to the crowd for Passover. But the crowd said, 'No! Release the rebel Barabbas instead.'

So here he hangs, deserted by nearly everyone because they're fearful of their own lives. A few women stand here with me and watch and wait. It's such a long, hot day. He's finding it hard to breathe now, gasping, every word an effort. So he doesn't say much.

He comforts one of the others up there on the cross with him. He tells his mother and his best friend to look after each other. What does his mother feel like, standing here? How hard it must be for her! But she is here, loving him, grieving for him.

How did the crowd change so? Only a few days ago they called him king, and bowed before him as he entered the city. Now they have thrown him out of the city, and his head is bowed in pain, beneath a mocking sign saying, 'Jesus of Nazareth, the king of the Jews'. How did it happen and why? What has he done to deserve this?

He called out to God to forgive the soldiers who hammered the nails in. He said they didn't know what they were doing. They're over on the side now, laughing and playing dice. Gambling over his few clothes, which are lying in a pile beneath the cross.

The crowd are laughing at him again. They're saying, 'You helped others, why can't you help yourself, and get down off that cross?' I can understand why one of his friends said he didn't know Jesus last night – not just once, but three times – when people asked him if he was with Jesus. The crowd has turned against Jesus, and all his friends are frightened.

It's getting near midday, and it's hot. My head hurts and my feet throb, standing here all these hours. But I can move about. He can't.

But now it's getting darker! People are looking up at the sky. It's the middle of the day, but suddenly it's getting as cold and dark as night. It's quiet; everyone's waiting. No more jeering, just people standing, quietly, waiting. This is different.

More time has passed. I can't move from here, not yet. It's three in the afternoon. It's close to the end now. He calls down that he's thirsty, and someone tries to give him a drink, from a sponge on a stick. Now he's shouting! Where did he get the strength? He shouts, 'God, don't abandon me!' Then his head goes down one last time. He's dead, even I can see that from here.

Suddenly the ground is shaking, rumbling all around us, like an earthquake. Rocks are splitting apart. People are shrieking, falling to the ground in fear. We are all terrified. Even the centurion in charge of the crucifixion. He's looking up at the cross, and he's saying, 'He really was the son of God.'

Dear God, what have we done?

Performance   This can be acted out as a mime, while the story is read. The children can be given the parts of Jesus, Simon, all those in the crowd around the cross, friends of Jesus, soldiers and mocking crowd.

Prayer   Dear God,
We remember those who are dying and those who have lost loved ones. Please bless them and help them in their time of need. Please help all those who are accused and punished unjustly. Amen.

A cross can be made out of cardboard and wood, and prayer requests and pictures, drawn in response to the story, could be pinned on to it.

General theme

How does it make us feel when someone, or a pet, dies? Let the children talk about ways of coping with death, but be sensitive to how this topic could affect some children.

Simon didn't want to carry the cross, but he did. Do we sometimes have to do things that we don't want to?

Did Jesus deserve to die? Do some crimes deserve the death penalty?

How does it feel when someone blames you for something you haven't done?

Christian theme

How do you think that the disciples felt, seeing Jesus die? What about all their hopes? Where was God?

Do we sometimes feel that God has let us down? How can we overcome that feeling?

Why did Jesus die?

Extension ideas

1. Make a stained glass window with a cross as a motif.
2. Write a story about a boy or girl being accused of something they did not do. What happens?
3. Simon carried a heavy load for Jesus. People caring for others who are ill long term also carry a heavy load. Think about what carers might need. Write about who might be a carer and what support they might need.
4. Jesus' execution was carried out according to Roman law, as they were controlling Israel at the time. The Romans also controlled parts of Britain. Do a project on the Roman occupation near you. What evidence is there now of their occupation (archeological, place names, etc.)? What was life like in Roman times in Britain?

Stephen's story:

Jesus lives again

References: Matthew 27:57–28:15; Mark 15:42–16:11; Luke 23:50–24:12; John 19:38–20:18

General theme: Lying or telling the truth?
Christian theme: Death has no power over Jesus.
Way in: Do you like surprises?
Introduction: This story is about a man called Stephen, who had a very big surprise, which he didn't like.

Story

One thing's for sure, they're going to blame me. It's not my fault, but that won't stop them. No one's going to believe me, and I don't blame them.

The body's gone. There, now you know. Where? Don't ask me. I know what they're saying though.

Look, all I know is that they brought his body down off the cross. That wealthy chap, Joseph of Arimathea, he convinced Pilate, the Roman governor, to give him the body. Some say he's a follower of Jesus, even though he's pretty well in with the Temple authorities. He has to be a follower really. Why else would he put himself out for this troublemaker, Jesus? Gave him his own tomb, and wrapped the body up in spices himself.

They had to do it quickly. Jesus had been executed on Friday, and the Sabbath day of rest begins on Friday evening. No one can do any work then.

Well, on Saturday, the chief priests said to Pilate, 'Look, this liar, Jesus, said when he was alive that he would come back to life three days after he died. We wouldn't put it past his followers to steal the body and pretend that he had come back to life. Let us guard his body until three days are up. Just to be on the safe side.'

Pilate gave the OK and that's where I come in. I'm in charge of the guards watching Jesus' tomb.

It was a big hole in the rock. The body was already inside when we got there and a huge stone had been rolled in front of it to block off the entrance.

The priests came and checked it was all as it should be. They added a seal to the stone in front of the tomb and left us to guard it. Quiet as anything it was on the Saturday. Well, as I said it was the Sabbath, wasn't it? No one's allowed to do anything, or even walk very far. So we had it very quiet. No one came near. We just sat there. Money for nothing, we thought. No followers would come to steal the body and Jesus was hardly likely to bother us was he?

That's what we thought. At dawn on Sunday, we saw two women coming towards the tomb. Before we could challenge them or anything, there was a terrific earthquake. There had been one on Friday, and now here was another one. The ground was shaking and there was a great rumbling noise. We were terrified.

Then things got really scary. You wouldn't think it could get worse, but believe me it could and it did. All of a sudden this being appeared. Never seen anything like it before. I guess it must have been an angel. He was white as snow and bright as lightning. I could hardly bear the brightness, I had to shield my face. Anyway this chap rolls the stone away, like it's a pebble, and then sits on it.

I lost it then, I don't mind telling you. I was shaking so I couldn't stand, and I dropped down to the ground. All of us did. Flat out on the ground.

The last thing I remember is the angel telling the women not to be afraid. He said that he knew they were looking for Jesus but that he wasn't in the tomb anymore. He'd come back to life and they would see him soon.

When I came to again, the women had gone. They must have run off. Well, wouldn't you? We could see the stone rolled away from the entrance, and when we plucked up the courage to look inside, we could see that the body had gone. There was just an empty tomb.

We spent the next few minutes arguing about what to do. Should we run away and hide, or try and get the stone back and pretend it never happened, or go and tell the priests? We decided to go and tell the priests. If there was going to be trouble, we wanted to get our side of the story in first.

We ran back to the priests. We told them how we'd done all that they had asked, but that this being from heaven had come down, and moved the stone, and that Jesus' body had disappeared. They went away and talked amongst themselves. They were none too pleased, I can tell you. When they came back they did the last thing any of us expected. We'd expected a flogging or some other punishment, but they loaded us up with money.

They said, 'Tell everyone his disciples came and stole the body in the night while you were asleep.'

We said, 'Oh, yes, and if the governor hears this we'll be in big trouble. We can be punished for falling asleep on duty.'

They said, 'If the governor hears about it, we'll tell him the truth – that you are innocent and didn't fall asleep. You don't need to worry.'

Well, what choice did we have really? The thing about those priests is that you don't want to annoy them. Look what happened to Jesus.

So we took the money and we were grateful for it. We went round telling anyone we could that his followers stole the body. But the women we'd seen had a different tale. They said that they'd met Jesus alive. And people are beginning to believe them.

Like I said, they'll blame me sooner or later for all of this. The priests don't really want to believe my story. But it's not my fault the body disappeared. I just wish I knew where it had gone.

Performance

This could be performed using puppets. Soldier's equipment, real or pretend, could be used as props.

Prayer

Dear God,
Thank you for happy surprises. Thank you that Jesus' story does not end on the cross. Thank you for the joy of Easter.
Amen.

The children could compose their own Easter song of praise, or learn a traditional Easter hymn.

General theme

Have you got examples of happy surprises, such as birthday treats or unexpected family visits? And unhappy surprises?
What about losing something or a friend moving away? How did you feel?
Not all surprises are happy. The friends of Jesus were happy; the guards and priests were not. How do you think they felt?
The guard was asked to tell a lie. Do you think he should have done so? Why or why not?
Is telling a lie ever the right thing to do? What do you think you would have done in the guard's position?

Christian theme

How do you think the friends of Jesus felt when they heard the news?

Jesus seemed to know what was going to happen. What does this tell us about his relationship with God?

Does the resurrection change how we look at the cross and death? If Jesus did come back to life, how does it change things?

Extension ideas

1. Plant a pip or seed and watch it grow. The seed has to die before the plant can grow.
2. Draw pictures of the four seasons, with the cycle of growth from winter into spring.
3. Write a story about a happy surprise, perhaps about a pet being found safe after being lost.
4. Some people make Easter gardens at Easter, or decorate twigs as Easter trees. Some make or give chocolates to each other. Easter cards often have eggs on them as a symbol of new life breaking out. Try to decorate eggs, make pictures of decorated eggs, or do one of the above to celebrate new life.

Jesus appears to his disciples

Reference: John 20:19-29

General theme: Seeing is believing.

Christian theme: Jesus changes Thomas' doubts into belief.

Way in: Have you ever felt left out? For example, have you ever not been able to go to a party or see a film? Perhaps you felt this way missing England score a goal?

Introduction: This story is about one of Jesus' friends, called Thomas, who missed something important, and felt left out.

Story   Grief does funny things to people. It can even make you think you've seen someone you love, when you know that they are dead. And we were sad, all of us. Tears all round, even from big strong men not used to showing emotion.

Jesus was dead. We missed him. He was our leader, we looked to him for advice, friendship and leadership. We felt like a boat without a rudder; no one knew what to do. We met together for comfort, and sat in rooms with the doors locked and bolted. They'd killed Jesus, who knew what they might do to us.

Jesus was dead and all our hopes had gone with him. We didn't always understand what he meant, or what he was up to, but he gave us hope. Now there was none.

So when the others told me that on the Sunday evening when they were all in the room together, doors locked, Jesus had just appeared in the middle of them, of course I didn't believe it was true. They said, 'Thomas, he was here, standing right there. He showed us his hands where the nails went in and his side, where the soldiers pierced him to make sure that he was dead. It was him. He looked different, but it was him.'

I have to say, they did look different. Before they'd looked like me, tired, gloomy and scared. Now their faces were shining with joy. They were excited and happy. But it couldn't be true. Jesus was dead.

They said, 'He told us not to be frightened. He even breathed on us, as though he was giving us his strength. And he told us that God had something special for us to do. We are to do God's work.'

Well it certainly sounded like the sort of thing he would say. But he was dead, so they must have imagined it.

I wasn't there, of course, when this happened. They came running to tell me as soon as I got back. There'd been rumours all day. Some women said his body had gone from the tomb, and that they had seen him. Others had said that they had seen him, even walked with him, and not recognised him at first, until he'd said grace over a meal.

Well it was all these sightings that made me think that it couldn't be true. He couldn't be everywhere could he?

I said, 'Well, lads, I know that you're excited, but unless I see the scars on his hand, and stick my finger in them, and put my hand into the hole in his side, I won't believe it.'

They tried to convince me, but I wouldn't change my mind. A long lonely week went by. It's hard when you're still feeling sad because your friend is dead, and everyone else is excited and saying that he's alive. You can't join in; you're on your own, moping in the corner. I wanted to believe, I really wanted to, but common sense told me that it couldn't be true. Someone had to stay practical in the middle of all this hysteria.

Anyway, a week later we were all together again, eating and chatting, still with the doors locked because we were still frightened of the authorities. And blow me down, he was suddenly there with us. In the middle of a locked room. He didn't come through the doors or windows, he didn't walk through the walls. He was just there, standing with us, with that smile on his face.

He wasn't a ghost. He was real, like us, but different somehow. All the pain that he'd gone through had left marks on him, but there was something else. He looked as though something wonderful had happened to him, as though he'd been given the biggest present you could imagine. He stood there looking all vulnerable with his scarred hands and feet, but at the same time he looked the strongest person I'd ever seen.

He gave us a greeting, 'Peace be with you.' Then he came over to me. I could feel my face going red as I remembered all the times that I'd said, 'Jesus is dead. Stop believing in fairy tales.' Now there he was in front of me, looking at me, half amused, half serious, as though he understood how much I was hurting.

'Thomas,' he said. 'Here I am. Look at my hands. Put your finger here, in the hole. Then to make sure it's me and I'm here, stick out your hand and pop it into that hole in my side, where the spear went in. Then maybe you'll stop your doubting and believe it's me.'

I looked. There was no doubt. He was as real as me. More real, I think. There was something about him that just oozed life and power. He seemed the most alive person I'd ever seen. I didn't need my fingers to tell me that he was here. I said the only thing that I could say: 'My Lord and my God.'

Then he said to me, 'Now you believe because you've seen me. Many others will be happy and believe without seeing me.'

We were the first witnesses to the unbelievable. Jesus was dead, but now he is alive.

Performance

This could be read by a narrator, with the speeches being read by other children.

Prayer

Dear God,
Thank you for friends. Thank you for the fun of sharing things with them. Please help us when we feel sad or left out and help us to help our friends when they feel sad.
Amen.

To celebrate the idea of no one being left out, the children could stand in a circle and each say, in turn, 'Thank you God for [name of person next to them].' If appropriate they could extend the prayer with a phrase, such as, because s/he always makes me laugh, because s/he is good at football, etc.

General theme

What things make us sad?
Thomas did not believe his friends. Have you ever not believed your friends when they have told you something? How did they feel when you did not believe them?
Thomas was sad because he felt left out, because the others had seen Jesus. How can we help people who feel left out?

Christian theme

How do you think Thomas felt after seeing Jesus?
The disciples were witnesses to Jesus being alive again, and they told everyone what they had seen. Can we be witnesses too? How?
The writer of Hebrews says in chapter 11, verses 1-2 that to have faith is to be sure of things we hope for, to be certain of the things we cannot see. Did Thomas have faith? What can we base our faith on?

Extension ideas

1. Paint a picture or make a collage of one of your friends.
2. There are many things that exist that we cannot see, some because they are too small to be seen with the naked eye. Have a look at things through a magnifying glass or a microscope.
3. Write a story about a boy/girl who sees something and no one believes them. What do they see – a robbery or someone being bullied? What happens next?
4. As a class, read all or part of *The Lion, The Witch and The Wardrobe* by C. S. Lewis, especially the death and resurrection of Aslan.

Simon Peter's story (2):

Friends again

Reference: John 18:15-18, 25-27 and John 21:1-19

General theme: Reconciliation.

Christian theme: A God of second chances.

Way in: Have you ever had arguments with your friends? Have they ever let you down, or have you ever let them down?

Introduction: This is a story about one of Jesus' friends called Simon Peter, and what happened to him after he let Jesus down.

Story   The night that they arrested Jesus was the worst night of my life. I let him down so badly. I fell asleep in the olive grove when he asked us to stay awake with him and keep him company. Then when that traitor Judas came up and Jesus was arrested, I got so angry that I attacked one of the guards – sliced his ear right off with my sword. Even that didn't please Jesus; he didn't want people hurt for him. I guess it wasn't the guard's fault; he was just following orders.

So Jesus was led away and I trailed behind him, watching him bullied and beaten, questioned and marched around. I hung around in the courtyards waiting. Jesus had told me earlier that night that I'd let him down, and I'd said, 'I'll never do that, Lord. Even if everybody else leaves you, I'll stay with you.'

He'd looked at me and said, 'Peter, before dawn comes up, and the cockerel has crowed, you'll have said three times that you don't know me.'

I said, 'Never. Even if I have to die.' But I didn't know what was coming. I didn't know how frightened I was going to be, seeing what they were doing to Jesus.

I was waiting in the courtyard, keeping warm by the fire because it was cold, when one of the servants there said, 'Hey, you were with Jesus, weren't you?'

I said, 'I don't know what you are talking about.'

But one of the others there had looked up and said, 'Yes, you were with Jesus.'

Trembling I said, 'I swear, I don't even know him.'

I went to stand by the gateway, in the cold and dark, out of the way. But a man came up and said, 'You were with the Galilean. You can't deny it, you have the same accent.'

I was scared, people were turning their heads and looking at me. I said, 'I don't know him. Leave me alone.' And then the cockerel crowed. I remembered what Jesus had said, and I went out into the dark and cried and cried. He knew I would let him down. He knew me better than I knew myself.

Well, it didn't get better, did it. They killed him. Then when we saw him again afterwards, when he came back to life, the others were all so excited. So was I, at least part of me was. Part of me felt guilty and ashamed that I'd let him down, when he needed me most. How could he ever love and trust me again? I couldn't be his friend now.

So I kept out of the way. I knew he wouldn't want me near him. I couldn't be trusted.

One day, just after he'd come back, we were feeling a bit bolder, and I wanted to get out of doors. We'd spent too much time locked up in rooms. I said to the others, 'I'm going fishing.'

Some of them said, 'We'll come with you.' So Thomas, Nathaniel, James, John, me and two other lads went down to Lake Tiberius to fish.

We were out all night, but we didn't even catch a tiddler. As dawn came, the sun came up over the lake and we could see someone at the water's edge. But we didn't know who it was. This chap shouted out, 'Caught anything, lads?'

'Not a thing,' we called back from the boat.

'Try chucking your net out on the right side and you'll catch something,' he said.

Well maybe he could see something from the water's edge that we couldn't, shadows of a shoal of fish in the water, against the sunlight, perhaps. So we tried and we made a big catch.

John said, 'How about that. I'll bet that's Jesus.'

When he said that, I thought, of course it is. I remembered he'd done something similar, when I first met him. I got so excited that I forgot that I'd let him down and I jumped into the water and swam for it. I left the others to bring the boat in.

When we got to the shore, Jesus was cooking our breakfast. He'd got a fire going on the beach and he was cooking fish. There was fresh bread nearby too. It smelt so good early in the morning, after a long, cold night fishing. Jesus looked up and said, 'Throw on some more fish. Some of your catch.' So we did.

He said, 'Come on over, lads, and get something to eat.' It all looked so normal, him tending the fire, squatting down on the stones. But to be honest, we were all a bit afraid of him, since he'd, you know, come back from the dead. So we didn't move. In the end, it was him who came to us. He walked over with a loaf of bread, broke it up and gave a bit of it to each of us. He did the same with the fish, because we still didn't move.

Then, after we'd eaten, Jesus suddenly said to me, in front of my mates, 'Simon do you love me more than the others do?'

What a question! I don't know how much they love him, do I? I just said, 'Yes, you know I love you.'

He said, 'Take care of my lambs.' What a strange thing to say. Then he asked again, 'Simon, do you love me?'

'Yes,' I said, 'You know I love you.'

'Look after my sheep,' said Jesus.

Before I'd had time to think about it, he asked a third time, 'Simon, do you love me?'

I felt sad then because it didn't seem as though he believed me. How could I make him understand? I said, 'I said, I love you. You know everything, surely you know this.'

Jesus said, 'Feed my sheep. I'm telling you something important. When you were young you had freedom and did what you wanted. When you are older you will lose that freedom, and you won't be able to do what you want.' He paused and then he said simply, 'Follow me.'

Then I understood – we were friends again. He was giving me a second chance. Three times I'd said that I didn't know him. Three times he'd made me tell him I loved him. Now he was telling me that I was his friend again and that I should carry on following him and doing what he asked. But he was warning me to be ready to suffer for him. People would make me a prisoner.

Before, I let him down. Now he's given me a second chance, and I'm ready. No matter what it costs.

Performance   While the narrator reads the story, a group of children could mime Peter's denial and the breakfast on the beach.

Prayer   Dear God,
Thank you that even when we make big mistakes you still love us and want us to be your friends. Help us to be able to forgive our friends when they hurt us, and to give them a second chance. Amen.

As an exercise in praying for peace and reconciliation, the children could think of areas and issues where reconciliation is needed. These could be listed on a board and prayed for regularly, thanking God when the answers come. These might be local gang disputes, division over the fox hunting debate, Northern Ireland and wars and conflicts.

General theme

If a friend lets you down, how do you feel and what do you do? What kind of world do you think we would have if no one was ever given a second chance?

If we hurt someone and they give us a second chance, how can we show them that we are their friends again?

Christian theme

Simon Peter felt that Jesus knew him better than he knew himself. How do you think that Jesus felt when Peter let him down? Peter was sorry that he hurt Jesus. Do you think that Jesus would have forgiven him even if he wasn't sorry?

Simon Peter was given a second chance by Jesus. How do you think he felt, and how do you think he used that chance? Check your answer for the second part of this question with the book of the Acts of the Apostles in the Bible.

Extension ideas

1. Write a poem about second chances.
2. Jesus and his disciples had a picnic on the beach. Have a picnic, indoors or outdoors as appropriate. Include the playing of cooperative games, or a treasure hunt in teams, or something else that can be done together and with cooperation.
3. Paint a picture or make a collage of a beach scene, or things found on a beach.
4. Many beaches are in danger of pollution or damage by tourists, development or erosion. Look at how beaches may be damaged and how they may be saved. Draw up a Beach Code of Good Behaviour (for example, take litter home, don't damage anything, etc.).

   Or

   Through the use of books and other means, choose a historical dispute that has been solved and where reconciliation has taken place, as in South Africa, trade disputes and the aftermath of wars. Discover what is needed for reconciliation to work.